Decarbonizing Freight Transport

Sarah Pfoser

Decarbonizing Freight Transport

Acceptance and Policy Implications

Sarah Pfoser
Logistikum Steyr
University of Applied Sciences Upper
Austria
Steyr, Austria

This thesis was financially supported by the Government of Upper Austria and the University of Applied Sciences Upper Austria within the funding programs "FTI Grundlagenforschung" & "Dissertationsprogramm der Fachhochschule OÖ 2019".

ISBN 978-3-658-37102-9   ISBN 978-3-658-37103-6   (eBook)
https://doi.org/10.1007/978-3-658-37103-6

Responsible Editor: Marija Kojic
This Springer Gabler imprint is published by the registered company Springer Fachmedien Wiesbaden GmbH part of Springer Nature.
The registered company address is: Abraham-Lincoln-Str. 46, 65189 Wiesbaden, Germany

Foreword of Supervisor

Climate change is affecting our today's and tomorrow's society and will significantly impact the entire freight transport sector by massive structural changes. The megatrend of decarbonizing our economy and logistics cannot be neglected. But which measures are best suited in this context to ensure that the climate targets defined by various political parties can actually be achieved? And what is the contribution of freight transport to this, or in what way are freight transport systems affected by this?

The dissertation of Sarah Pfoser is embedded in this highly relevant research area and deals with this topic from different perspectives. As Ms. Pfoser's work clearly demonstrates, it is not enough to replace conventional fuels with alternative fuels in order to implement sustainable transport chains. The reduction of greenhouse gas emissions can only be achieved through the intelligent combination of modern information technologies, fuel substitution and modern cooperative organizational measures.

To transform freight transports to sustainable systems it is necessary to employ IT systems in order to consolidate traffic streams and additionally introduce horizontal cooperation. Essentially, the simultaneous avoidance, shift and improvement of freight transport needs to be targeted. Consequently, this dissertation examines the determinants which positively influence the acceptance of sustainable freight transport concepts and which reduce the overall negative impact of freight transport.

In this light, the work of Ms. Pfoser represents a successful interplay of micro-, macro- and meta-logistic levels of observation. Tomorrow's freight transports can only be sustainable—in an ecological sense—if each individual actor in the overall system recognizes the necessity of changing. Furthermore, the external framework conditions need to reward the implementation of decarbonization measures and need to encourage the joint implementation of decarbonization targets.

The cumulative dissertation comprises four journal publications that address the aforementioned aspects using a mixture of qualitative and quantitative methods. It is demonstrated that the use of the Physical Internet has a positive impact on sustainable logistics. In this context, a central orchestration of resources plays a significant role to promote sustainable solutions. It is also shown that sustainable transport concepts must rely on multimodality and that the share of rail and waterborne transport must be much higher than it is today. Ms. Pfoser's thesis clearly shows the underlying barriers in this regard and proposes measures to reduce these obstacles. The dissertation also addresses the possibility of using LNG as an alternative fuel in general and how the shift to this bridge fuel can be achieved.

Kudos for this work by Ms Pfoser, not only because she participated in the scientific discourse at an early stage of her career, but also as she impressively demonstrates a methodological and theoretical pluralism. This work contributes to a subject which is still in its infancy and which will have a significant impact in our future. With the expertise she has gained and her tenacity, I am convinced that the comprehensive knowledge generated by Ms. Pfoser will be highly recognized not only in science and practice, but also from a political perspective.

Bremen   Prof. Dr. Herbert Kotzab
23.01.2021

Preface

Writing a doctoral thesis is no sprint; instead it's a marathon consisting of a lot of small steps (or a long-haul delivery with many stopovers, since this thesis is written in the field of logistics). To be honest, I cannot say exactly when I started to run this marathon. I commenced doing research in 2013 with the simple objective of acquiring new knowledge within our research projects and sharing it with the research community. From the very beginning I was dedicated to the topic of sustainable freight transport, as I felt a personal passion for this research area. I did several research projects dealing with different strategies to decarbonize freight transport—among them the Physical Internet, multimodality and LNG. At a certain point in time I started to realize that there are clear patterns across these different strategies. I had talked to a lot of different logistics companies and I felt that no matter if I was asking them about horizontal collaboration or about a new technology such as LNG, they gave me similar opinions and answers about their acceptance of the strategies. This was the motivation to write this thesis— I wanted to put down all these patterns that I observed and derive implications about the general acceptance of sustainable freight transport. I feel that one of my main functions as a researcher is to support policy makers. Therefore I intended to develop policy recommendations based on my findings. These policy recommendations reflect the true requirements of the "users" of transport as they were developed in a process of collaboration with the logistics companies. It is obvious that policy measures are much more effective if they meet the needs of those who are targeted by the measures. The underlying idea was therefore to involve those who are targeted, i.e. the logistics companies, to create user-centric measures. The result is a set of applicable measures which promote the implementation of sustainable freight transport. The close collaboration with Austrian policy makers (Ministry of Transport (BMK) and the State of Upper Austria) throughout all of the research projects ensures that the recommendations are forwarded to the responsible parties. My greatest practical success was the scientific support of the construction of the first LNG fueling station in Austria in 2017 and the shift of road transport to multimodal rail transport by an Austrian plastics enterprise in 2019. Hopefully this was just the beginning and this thesis may encourage even more practitioners and scientists to promote sustainable freight transport practices, because we only have one earth and there is no planet B!

Danksagung

An erster Stelle möchte ich meinem Betreuer und Hauptgutachter Prof. Dr. Herbert Kotzab danken. Er gab mir einerseits den nötigen Freiraum bei der Ausarbeitung dieser Dissertation, war jedoch immer zur Stelle wenn ich ihn brauchte und hat mir mit hilfreichen Ratschlägen (und strengen Worten an gewisse Editoren) zahlreiche Male weitergeholfen. Er war es auch, der mich zu einer kumulativen Dissertation ermutigt hat – eine Entscheidung, über die ich heute noch sehr froh bin. Ich dank' Ihnen recht sakrisch, wie es bei uns so schön auf gut Österreichisch heißt! Darüber hinaus möchte ich Prof. Dr. Dr. h.c. Hans-Dietrich Haasis für die Übernahme des Zweitgutachtens dieser Dissertation danken.

Des Weiteren bedanke ich mich vielmals bei meinen Vorgesetzten Oliver Schauer und Lisa-Maria Putz, die mir in meiner bisherigen Laufbahn an der Fachhochschule Oberösterreich sehr viel ermöglicht haben und sich stets für mich eingesetzt haben. Lisa-Maria hat in vielerlei Hinsicht den Weg geebnet für uns nachfolgende Dissertanten, und sie hat mir während des gesamten Dissertationsprozesses durch das Teilen ihrer eigenen Erfahrungen weitergeholfen. Oliver bereichert unsere Publikationen und Forschungsprojekte insbesondere mit seinem praktischen Blick auf die Dinge, der auf seine außerordentlich wertvolle Wirtschaftserfahrung zurückzuführen ist. Nach einem Gespräch mit euch beiden bin ich immer klüger! Ohne eure Unterstützung und euer Vertrauen in meine Arbeit hätte ich die Zielgerade dieser Dissertation nicht erreicht – vielen Dank!

An dieser Stelle dürfen auch meine Ko-Autor*innen nicht fehlen, etwa Yasel Costa, der mich in die quantitative Forschungswelt eingeführt hat, und allen voran Michael Plasch, der mit mir eine 2,5-jährige Reise namens JBL-Einreichung angetreten hat. Wir haben in dieser Zeit beide sehr viel gelernt und uns sehr stark weiterentwickelt. Ich kann dir nur zustimmen, dass ich mir nach dieser langen Zeit gar nicht mehr vorstellen kann, eine Revision-Runde ohne dich durchzuboxen!

Dank gebührt auch den studentischen Mitarbeiter*innen Verena Stockhammer, Andrea Buchbauer und Thomas Berger, die mich im Laufe der letzten Jahre bei meinen Forschungsprojekten unterstützt und mich wesentlich entlastet haben, sodass ich die zeitlichen Kapazitäten für das Ausarbeiten der Dissertation zusammenkratzen konnte.

Besonders großer Dank geht insbesondere auch an meine Kammerl-Gefährten Christina Flitsch und Matthias Winter, die immer ein offenes Ohr für mich haben und mit denen ich sehr, sehr gerne die Freuden und Sorgen des Dissertantendaseins geteilt habe. Nicht zuletzt habt ihr stets für die notwendige Zerstreuung gesorgt, sei es beim Klettern oder bei anderen Aktivitäten abseits der Arbeit. Dies gilt auch für meinen „Brudi" Christian, der mir in diversen abendlichen interdisziplinären Strategiemeetings und auch in zahlreichen Brettspielwelt-Sessions geholfen hat, den Kopf frei zu bekommen. Großer Dank geht überdies an Simon Weger fürs „Flügel heben" in den letzten zehn Jahren.

Ganz spezieller Dank geht an meine bessere Hälfte, Gernot Mayr, der zurecht des Öfteren als mein „Ruhepol" bezeichnet wird und diese Funktion auch in den angespanntesten Phasen der Dissertation perfekt erfüllt hat. Seine Ausgeglichenheit und unerschöpfliche Geduld haben schon viele verblüfft, und nicht einmal meine Dissertationslaunen konnten daran etwas ändern. Ich bin sehr froh, dass wir uns gefunden haben!

Abschließend möchte ich meine allergrößte Dankbarkeit gegenüber meinen Eltern ausdrücken, die mich mit besonderer Fürsorge unterstützen und immerzu an mich glauben. Ihr habt immer schon sehr gut einschätzen können, was gut für mich ist, und ihr habt auch bei meiner Arbeit in der Forschung recht behalten! Ich widme euch daher diese Arbeit.

Steyr   Sarah Pfoser
November 2021

Abstract

One of the grand challenges the logistics industry is facing today is the question of how to limit the negative impact of freight transport. Freight transport demand is continuously rising and must be satisfied by logistics. The ever-increasing share of trucks is problematic due to the high external costs of road transport. European politics has dedicated itself to these problems and shows strong commitment to decarbonize logistics. For example, policy action plans are released and emission limits are set.

Despite the political endeavors, the environmental performance of the transport system has not improved so far. It seems that the existing measures are not sufficient to motivate transport users to implement sustainable freight transport strategies. Without transport users' willingness to realize sustainable freight transport, the strategies will fail. As a matter of fact, studies on transport users' demand for sustainable freight transport strategies are scarce. It is therefore difficult to consider their needs and requirements towards sustainable freight transport. To address this gap and promote sustainable practices, this thesis studies the acceptance of sustainable freight transport. Knowing the determinants of acceptance makes it possible to design measures which attract transport users to implement sustainable freight transport and help decarbonize logistics.

By involving a number of logistics companies (i.e. the users of the transport system), a user-centric perspective is ensured in this thesis. The idea is to gain a profound understanding of logistics companies' needs and requirements by studying their sustainable freight transport acceptance. Knowing the determinants of acceptance makes it possible to design policy measures which attract logistics companies to implement sustainable freight transport methods and help decarbonize logistics.

The case of three different strategies for sustainable freight transport is studied in the thesis: (1) horizontal collaboration in a Physical Internet network, (2) multimodal freight transport and (3) liquefied natural gas (LNG) as alternative truck fuel. Each of these three strategies falls within a different pillar of the avoid-shift-reduce framework. The avoid-shift-reduce framework is a well-known approach to classify sustainable transport strategies. Horizontal collaboration aims to *avoid* transport by enabling the bundling of transport streams and by increasing the utilization of transport capacities. Multimodal transport aims to *shift* freight to sustainable transport modes. And finally, LNG is a technological solution which aims to *improve* the environmental impact of road transport.

Studying the acceptance of sustainable freight transport revealed that there are different stages of acceptance which involve a varying degree of commitment by transport users. In context of this thesis, acceptance refers to the stages of willingness to use or the actual use of sustainable freight transport strategies. Within the empirical investigation (in-depth interviews, online survey), five main determinants were identified which influence the acceptance of the above mentioned avoid, shift and improve strategies. These determinants are profitability, customer demand, availability of infrastructure, organizational efforts and legal framework. Theoretical support for these determinants comes from the technology acceptance model.

Later on it is reported that severe market failures exist which inhibit the efficient diffusion of sustainable transport strategies. Logistics companies need an incentive to introduce sustainable freight transport. Currently they do not have an incentive because they do not (exclusively) benefit from the positive effects of introducing sustainable freight transport (tragedy of the commons). Even worse, they are not called to account for the negative externalities they produce. In some cases, insufficient information prevents the implementation of sustainable freight transport.

As the above mentioned market failures exist, it cannot be expected that sustainable transport strategies will be efficiently implemented without any policy intervention. For sustainable transport strategies to be diffused at a sufficient scale and speed, it will therefore be necessary to set suitable policy measures. Based on the information collected on the determinants of acceptance and existing market failures, policy measures are hence developed. Again, a user-centric approach is applied as logistics companies are involved in interviews and focus groups. This gives them the opportunity to bring in their opinion and needs. Theoretical support for the developed policy measures is derived from various organizational theories. According to these theories, the implementation of sustainable practices may either result from organizational obligations, organizational capabilities or organizational functioning.

To classify the developed policy measures, a new typology is developed. The reason is that the existing sticks-carrots-sermons typology falls short in a user-centric context. This is due to the fact that logistics companies do not favor restrictive command and control measures ("sticks"). Instead, they require "means", i.e. appropriate infrastructure and framework conditions, which support them with introducing sustainable freight transport. Infrastructure development, information & transparency and the adaptation of the legal framework constitute means. Beside means, transport users desire monetary incentives ("carrots") to ensure that the investment for sustainable freight transport is cost-efficient. The third type of policy measures ("sermons") refers to awareness raising activities or education & training. The intention of sermons is to create knowledge and consciousness for sustainable freight transport.

It is well known that whether an innovation will be accepted or rejected by its target group depends heavily on the way that user needs are integrated in the development of this innovation. The determinants of acceptance and suggested policy measures in this thesis reflect transport users' needs towards sustainable freight transport. This should support policy makers and the logistics industry to implement sustainable practices and achieve the ambitious emission targets by decarbonizing freight transport.

List of Publications of the Cumulative Thesis

PAPER I

Plasch, Michael; Pfoser, Sarah; Gerschberger, Markus; Schauer, Oliver; Gattringer, Regina (2021): Why collaborate in a Physical Internet network?—Motives and success factors. In *Journal of Business Logistics*. DOI: 10.1111/jbl.12260.

PAPER II

Pfoser, Sarah (in press): Developing user-centered measures to increase the share of multimodal freight transport. In Research in Transportation Business & Management. Available online: 29.10.2021. DOI: 10.1016/j.rtbm.2021.100729.

PAPER III

Pfoser, Sarah; Schauer, Oliver; Costa, Yasel (2018): Acceptance of LNG as an alternative fuel: Determinants and policy implications. In *Energy Policy* 120, pp. 259–267. DOI: 10.1016/j.enpol.2018.05.046.

PAPER IV

Pfoser, Sarah; Aschauer, Gerald; Simmer, Laura; Schauer, Oliver (2016): Facilitating the implementation of LNG as an alternative fuel technology in landlocked Europe: A study from Austria. In *Research in Transportation Business & Management* 18, pp. 77–84. DOI: 10.1016/j.rtbm.2016.01.004.

Contents

Abbreviations

ASI	Avoid shift improve
CNG	Compressed natural gas
CO_2	Carbon dioxide
EU	European Union
GHG	Greenhouse gas emissions
GLEC	Global Logistics Emissions Council
H2	Hydrogen
HGV	Heavy goods vehicle
ICT	Information and communication technology
ITS	Intelligent transport services
LNG	Liquefied natural gas
LSP	Logistics service provider
NO_x	Nitrogen oxide
PI	Physical Internet
PM	Particulate matter
R&D	Research and development
RQ	Research question
SCM	Supply chain management
SO_x	Sulfur oxide
tkm	ton kilometers
TRA	Theory of reasoned action
UNFCCC	United Nations Framework Convention on Climate Change
WTW	Well-to-wheel

List of Figures

List of Tables

Introduction

1

1.1 Motivation and Background

Logistics processes typically involve a high number of resources and activities which have a substantial impact on the sustainability performance of an organization. The most relevant logistics activity with the highest impact on sustainability is without a doubt transportation (Bretzke, 2011). As a matter of fact, the transport sector is one of the highest energy consuming and highest emission causing sectors (European Commission, 2011). However, the transport sector is key to delivering economic growth. Recent changes in customers' expectations have shown significant changes in consumer behavior. Services such as same-day-deliveries and free return of goods have become natural prerequisites in e-commerce (Morganti *et al.*, 2014). In B2B relations, just-in-time or even just-in-sequence deliveries have become common practice in specific industries such as automotive (Battini *et al.*, 2013). These developments result in growing freight volumes which have to be managed by logistics. Figure 1.1 shows the trend of increasing freight volumes. It can be seen that current freight volumes are considerably higher than two decades ago. Figure 1.1 also illustrates the modal split of freight transport at intra-EU level, where road transport has the highest share at slightly more than 50%, followed by a relatively high share of maritime transport (30%). In inland freight transport, the share of road transport is even higher, at around 75% (European Commission, 2019). This means that three quarters of the inland freight transport is carried out on roads, thus leaving a significant environmental footprint.

© The Author(s) 2022
S. Pfoser, *Decarbonizing Freight Transport*,
https://doi.org/10.1007/978-3-658-37103-6_1

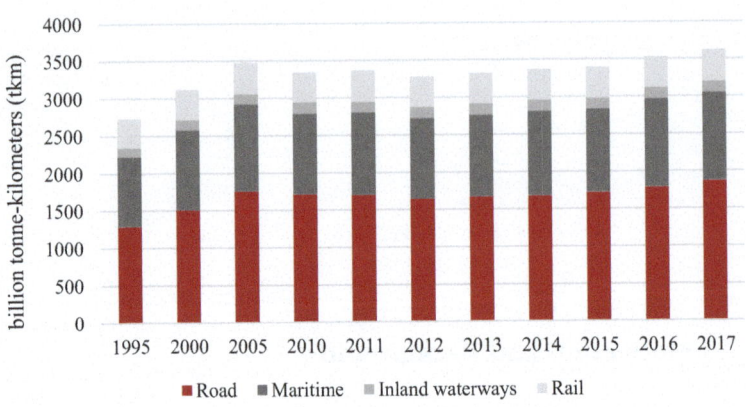

Figure 1.1   Freight transport volume and modal split within the EU. (data from European Environment Agency, 2019a)

It is projected that the environmental problems will even continue to grow within the next decades; in particular the share of road transport is predicted to rise further (McKinnon *et al.*, 2015). This is critical because road transport causes a lot of negative effects compared to other transport modes, not only emissions, but also other external costs such as noise, congestion or accidents. Figure 1.2 summarizes the external costs of road transport, rail transport and inland waterway transport. The external costs of road transport amount to 2.01 cent per ton-kilometer and thus are substantially higher than the external costs of railway transport (0.80 cent per ton-kilometer) and inland waterways (0.27 cent per ton-kilometer).

In view of these statistics and recent developments, it becomes evident that measures have to be taken to counteract the negative environmental performance of freight transport. For quite a long time, governments all over Europe have recognized the environmental harm of the transport sector and have committed themselves towards sustainable development as a policy goal. This has resulted in a vast number of national and international strategies, environmental conventions as well as regional development programs (Howes *et al.*, 2017). On the global level, the Paris Agreement (UNFCCC, 2016) was a key milestone for world-wide climate policy. The Paris Agreement was adopted by the United Nations Framework Convention on Climate Change (UNFCCC) at the Paris climate conference (COP21) in December 2015. It is the first binding agreement that sets a specific

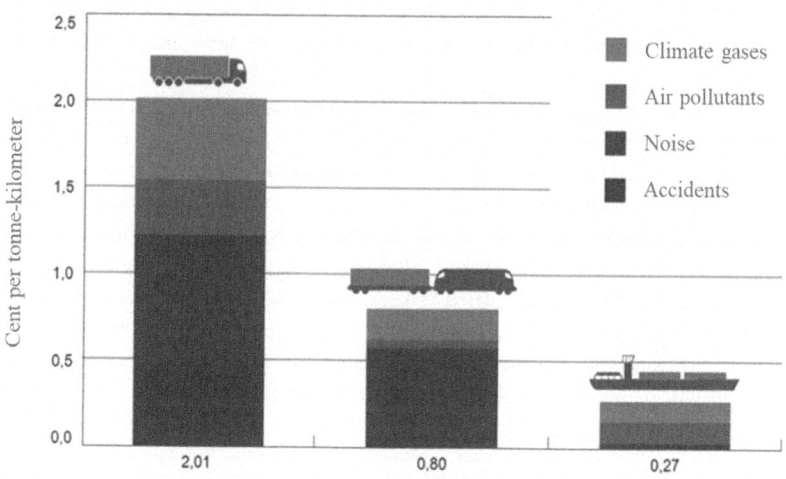

Figure 1.2 Sum of external costs for different transport modes. (average values for selected transports of bulk goods, via donau, 2019)

limit for global warming. The aim is to combat climate change by keeping global warming to well below 2 °C (UNFCCC, 2016). Compared to the preceding Kyoto Protocol, the Paris Agreement is an important step forward as it involves the commitment of 195 contractual parties. The Kyoto Protocol only targeted industrial countries (and only those which ratified the convention).

In accordance with the Paris Agreement, each party has to set measures to comply with the climate targets. Europe has taken a leading role as it aims to become the first climate-neutral continent. For that purpose, the European Green Deal was released, which provides an ambitious action plan to ensure that there are no net emissions of greenhouse gases by 2050. The action plan includes measures to facilitate the efficient use of resources by advancing towards a circular economy. Biodiversity should be restored and emissions should be cut. It is intended to convert the political commitment into a legally binding obligation to ensure that the Green Deal does not turn into empty promises. A proposal for a European Climate Law (COM(2020) 80 final) has been developed, which aims to write into law the goal to become the first climate-neutral continent. The law involves measures to keep track of progress and enables the adjustment of actions to reach the targets. In accordance with the global stock take exercise set out in the Paris Agreement, progress should be analyzed every five years.

To realize the goals of the European Green Deal, transport emissions will need to be reduced dramatically. This is a challenging task since global transport demand is predicted to triple by the year of 2050, which would result in twice as many carbon emissions (International Transport Forum, 2019). An ambitious roadmap published by the European Technology Platform ALICE suggests a framework to reduce all logistics-related emissions to zero by 2050 (Punte *et al.*, 2019). Efficiency gains should be leveraged to better use transport capacities and increase the productivity of the whole freight system. The deployment of sustainable vehicle technologies should additionally support the decarbonization of freight transport (Punte *et al.*, 2019). The ALICE roadmap towards zero emission logistics is indisputably an important step towards green and sustainable future logistics. However, it remains unclear whether the measures suggested in this roadmap will be accepted and enforced by the relevant stakeholders.

1.2   Research Gap and Objectives

Despite the intense political endeavors described above, the environmental performance of the transport system has not improved so far (Islam *et al.*, 2016; European Commission, 2019). It seems that existing measures are not sufficient to motivate transport users to implement sustainable freight transport strategies. To set measures which efficiently encourage the introduction of sustainable freight transport, the demand for and acceptance of sustainable freight transport must be understood. Without transport users' demand for environmental transport practices, sustainable freight transport will fail (Lindholm and Blinge, 2014). It is therefore important that policy measures address the needs of transport users and promote their demand for sustainable freight transport.

Many different alternatives exist to realize sustainable freight transport, but studies on the demand for these alternatives are scarce. In the course of this thesis, three sustainable freight transport strategies will be discussed in detail. These three strategies are horizontal collaboration in a Physical Internet (PI) network, multimodal freight transport and Liquefied Natural Gas (LNG) as alternative fuel. Each of these three strategies contributes in a different way to the goal of reducing greenhouse gas emissions from freight transport. Horizontal collaboration aims to avoid transport by enabling the bundling of transport streams and by increasing the utilization of transport capacities. Multimodal transport aims to shift freight to sustainable transport modes. And finally, LNG is a technological solution which aims to improve the environmental impact of road transport.

Considerable research has already been conducted on each of these three sustainable freight transport strategies. However, the majority of publications focus on the *supply* of these three sustainable strategies. The following Table 1.1 gives an overview of supply-related literature on the three strategies.

Table 1.1 Studies on the supply of sustainable transport strategies

Sustainable transport strategy	Supply-related topics covered in the literature	References
Horizontal collaboration & transport bundling in a PI network	Design and use of containers in the PI network: standardization, modularization, handling cost, intelligent containers,...	Hofman *et al.* (2016), Sallez *et al.* (2015), Landschützer *et al.* (2015), Lin *et al.* (2014)
	Inventory problems in the PI network: optimized inventory levels, warehousing services, reduced inventory costs, maximized utilization,...	Ji *et al.* (2019), Yang *et al.* (2017), Darvish *et al.* (2016), Pan *et al.* (2015)
	Distribution and transport in the PI network: network optimization, optimized routing, loading patterns, truck scheduling,...	Chargui *et al.* (2020), Ji *et al.* (2019), Gontara *et al.* (2018), Fazili *et al.* (2017), Tran-Dang *et al.* (2017), Venkatadri *et al.* (2016), Walha *et al.* (2016)
	Dynamic pricing and auction trading in the PI network	Qiao *et al.* (2019), Qiao *et al.* (2018), van Riessen *et al.* (2017), Kong *et al.* (2016)
Multimodal freight transport	Multimodal transport terminals: Hub location, hub design,..	Osorio-Mora *et al.* (2020), Li and Wang (2018),Kumar and Anbanandam (2019), Karimi and Bashiri (2018)
	Multimodal transport scheduling: optimum routing, transshipment, time constraints,...	Abbassi *et al.* (2019), Wolfinger *et al.* (2019), Layeb *et al.* (2018), Ghaderi *et al.* (2016), Le Li *et al.* (2015)
	Multimodal pricing: cost allocation and pricing schemes,....	Zheng *et al.* (2016), Kordnejad (2014), Shi and Li (2010)
LNG as an alternative fuel	Vehicle technology: pressure of LNG vehicles, vehicle design,...	Yonggang *et al.* (2013), Shangbing (2009), Wiens *et al.* (2001)

(continued)

Table 1.1 (continued)

Sustainable transport strategy	Supply-related topics covered in the literature	References
	Fueling systems: tank technology, refueling station design,...	Deng *et al.* (2019), Zhou (2011), Xiaodong and Wang Shunhua (2009), Xie *et al.* (2007), Chen *et al.* (2004)
	Safety in LNG operations: safety at storage facilities,..	Aneziris *et al.* (2020), Li (2019), Zhu (2011), Chun (2010)
	Lifecycle analyses of LNG applications	Langshaw *et al.* (2020), Xunmin (2019), Song *et al.* (2017), Arteconi *et al.* (2010)

As can be seen in Table 1.1, a multitude of topics associated with the supply of sustainable freight transport is covered by the literature. The literature on PI indicates how to design and use containers in the PI, how to solve inventory problems in the PI, how to optimize distribution and transport and how to price PI services. All of these topics are important for the supply of PI services. Similarly, the multimodal literature supports multimodal terminal design, multimodal transport scheduling and multimodal pricing. Again, these questions are related to the supply of multimodal services. And finally, the LNG literature specifies the LNG vehicle technology, fueling systems, safety in LNG operations and it provides lifecycle analyses—all of which is relevant to supply LNG.

All of the topics listed in Table 1.1 are undoubtedly important for the provision and implementation of sustainable freight transport. However, these topics mostly neglect the transport users' perspective and needs. As explained above, sustainable freight transport will not be implemented without transport users' demand to do so. As a matter of fact, studies on transport users' demand of the aforementioned three sustainable freight transport strategies are scarce. Kim *et al.* (2017) was critical about the fact that few studies consider the relationship between demand-side characteristics and the choice of transport services. Perboli *et al.* (2017) deal with horizontal logistics collaboration (synchromodality, a preliminary stage of PI) and find that existing literature is very much focused on the technical, ICT and optimization issues. This finding was confirmed by Pfoser *et al.* (in press), where a comprehensive literature review of 85 publications on synchromodality was conducted. Out of these 85 publications, hardly any study focuses on demand-side questions of horizontal logistics collaboration. Literature reviews on multimodal freight transport come to the same conclusion. SteadieSeifi *et al.* (2014) and Agamez-Arias and Moyano-Fuentes (2017) clearly show that multimodal literature predominantly deals with multimodal freight transportation planning, i.e. the optimization of multimodal service supply. Finally, the same can be said for LNG as an alternative fuel. Osorio-Tejada *et al.* (2017, p. 790) write that "the main difficulties for the deployment of LNG-fueled trucks are market related". Further research is therefore needed to evaluate the requirements of the market and the demand conditions for LNG.

The excessive focus on technological and supply-related questions of sustainable freight transport bears the risk of designing services and concepts which are not matching with the industrial needs (Perboli *et al.*, 2017). As illustrated above, there is a clear lack of market-related research on the demand for sustainable freight transport. This thesis contributes to the larger body of literature by providing insights into the demand for sustainable freight transport. The acceptance of an innovation is an important precondition and first step of the demand for this innovation (Dillon and Morris, 1996). Since many strategies for sustainable freight transport are in an early development stage, acceptance of these strategies must emerge before they can find widespread application and demand (McKinnon, 2018). The thesis therefore aims to analyze the determinants of sustainable freight transport acceptance. The intention is to understand acceptance in order to be able to propose measures to influence acceptance (and finally demand) for sustainable freight transport. Knowing the determinants of acceptance allows the design of measures which attract transport users to implement sustainable freight transport and help decarbonize logistics.

Based on the research gap described above, two main objectives can be derived for this thesis (Figure 1.3). The first objective is to analyze the determinants of transport users' sustainable freight transport acceptance. The second objective is to develop user-centric policy measures which promote the implementation of sustainable freight transport.

Both objectives of this thesis aim to advance the diffusion of sustainable freight transport. The objectives refer to different steps in the innovation diffusion process described by Reusswig *et al.* (2004) (see Figure 1.3): the first objective is related to the acceptance step which involves users' demand for sustainable freight transport. While many authors claim to have measured acceptance (see list of acceptance studies later in Section 5.1.3), they barely deliver a profound understanding of what actually influences acceptance and what leads to increased acceptance (Adell *et al.*, 2018). It is therefore an important contribution of this thesis to deliver an understanding of users' profound needs and requirements towards the introduction of sustainable freight transport. The second objective is related to the implementation step since the developed policy measures target

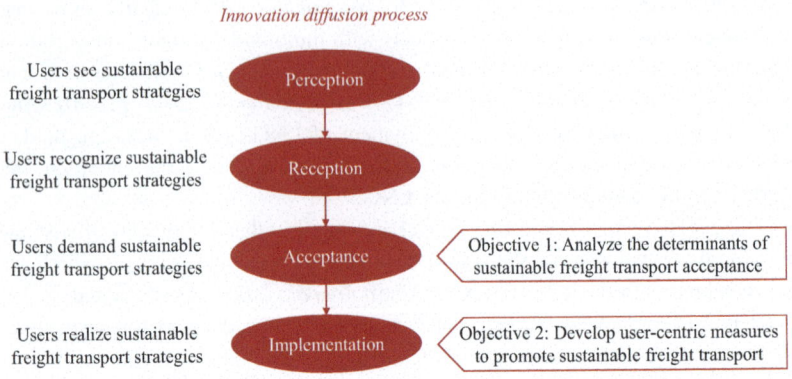

Figure 1.3 Innovation diffusion process and related objectives of the thesis. (own illustration based on Reusswig *et al.*, 2004)

the implementation of sustainable freight transport. The development of policy measures is based on the previously defined determinants of sustainable freight transport acceptance. According to Mattauch *et al.* (2016), demand-side regulations have been recommended to be effective by transport research for a long time. Therefore, the acceptance for sustainable freight transport will be analyzed in this thesis to develop measures which precisely address the requirements of the demand side. To summarize, the overall motivation of this thesis is to encourage the diffusion of sustainable freight transport by gaining an understanding for the acceptance of sustainable freight transport and suggesting suitable policy measures.

1.3   Structure and Research Questions

In this thesis, three different strategies for sustainable freight transport are under investigation, namely (1) horizontal collaboration in a PI network (2) multimodal freight transport and (3) LNG as an alternative fuel. Each of the three strategies falls within another pillar of the common ASI (avoid-shift-improve) framework. The ASI framework is widely used to structure strategies for sustainable transport. The fact that this thesis covers all three ASI pillars allows the comparison of the similarities and differences that exist between the different types of strategies.

As stated above, the objective of the thesis is first to study the acceptance of three specific sustainable freight transport strategies, and then develop policy measures which promote sustainable freight transport. The cases of the three sustainable freight transport strategies (PI collaboration, multimodality, LNG) were studied in detail within different research projects where the author of this thesis was involved in recent years. The findings of the three cases reveal the determinants of acceptance and policy measures to promote the three strategies for sustainable freight transport. These findings are summarized in various publications, which form the basis of this cumulative thesis (Figure 1.4). The aim of the present manuscript is to juxtapose the results of the individual publications and evaluate the patterns among the three strategies. This results in a list of overarching determinants which influence the acceptance of sustainable freight transport in general as well as overarching policy measures which are suitable to promote sustainable freight transport in general.

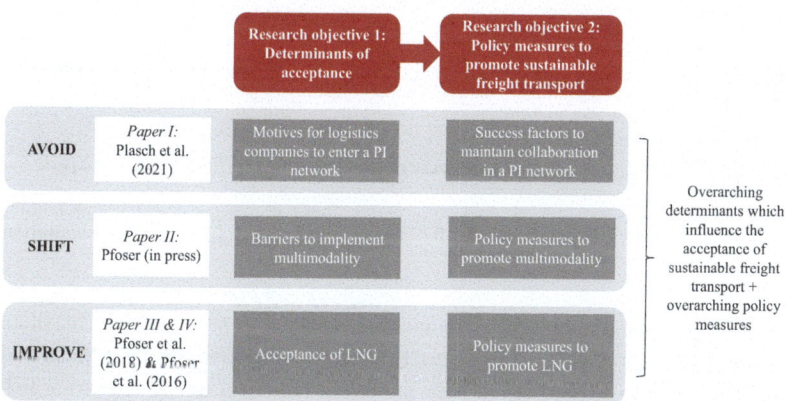

Figure 1.4   Structure of the thesis

The four papers contribute to answer the research questions underlying this thesis. The first research question aims to explain why PI collaboration, multimodality and LNG have been chosen as sustainability strategies under investigation in this thesis:

RQ 1: Which sustainable freight transport strategies exist to reduce the negative environmental impact of freight transport?

RQ 1 will be answered in Chapter 4 "Strategies for sustainable freight transport". Here, an introduction of the ASI-framework will be given to present a classification of sustainable freight transport strategies. Afterwards, three particular strategies (each representing a different ASI pillar) will be introduced in detail. As mentioned above, these three strategies are horizontal collaboration in a PI (avoid pillar), multimodality (shift pillar) and LNG as an alternative fuel (improve pillar).

The subsequent second research question refers to the acceptance of the three sustainable freight transport strategies under investigation in this thesis and contains three sub research questions:

RQ 2: Which determinants influence the acceptance of sustainable freight transport strategies?

RQ 2.1: Which motives support the acceptance of horizontal collaboration in a PI network?

RQ 2.2: Which barriers prevent the acceptance of multimodal freight transport?

RQ 2.3: Which determinants influence the acceptance of LNG as an alternative fuel?

The three sub research questions are answered in the four papers which constitute this thesis. Plasch *et al.* (2021) [Paper I] analyze the motives to enter horizontal collaboration in a PI network. These motives are defined as the reasons which encourage logistics companies to become part of the PI network. The motives determine the demand for PI collaboration, and as such they represent the determinants of PI acceptance (RQ 2.1). Pfoser (in press) [Paper II] evaluates the barriers to multimodal freight transport. Detailed insights into logistics companies' considerations of multimodality are given. From these insights, conclusions can be drawn about the determinants of multimodal freight transport acceptance to answer RQ 2.2. Pfoser *et al.* (2018d) [Paper III] show the determinants of LNG acceptance, which answers RQ 2.3. Additional insights about the acceptance of LNG are included from another paper, namely Pfoser *et al.* (2016a) [PAPER IV]. In Subchapter 3.3 "Determinants of sustainable freight transport acceptance", the results of the sub research questions 2.1 – 2.3 are merged to answer the overarching RQ 2 and summarize the determinants of sustainable freight transport acceptance.

Assuming rational behavior of decision makers, sustainable freight transport strategies should be used much more than it is currently the case since they increase the efficiency (as they decrease the emissions) of the whole logistics system (McKinnon *et al.*, 2015). The hesitant use of sustainable strategies suggests that market failures exist which distort the acceptance of sustainable strategies at present (Engel and Saleska, 2005; Sinnandavar *et al.*, 2018). The third research question will therefore examine:

RQ 3: Which market failures currently distort the acceptance of sustainable freight transport?

RQ 3 will be answered in Subchapter 4.3 "Market failures in sustainable freight transport". A number of market failures will be presented which result from the empirical investigation in this thesis. These market failures represent a relevant basis for the development of policy measures since policy measures should target the elimination of the market failures (Pindyck and Rubinfeld, 2013).

The fourth and final research question comes along with three sub research questions to develop policy measures for sustainable freight transport:

RQ 4: Which policy measures promote the implementation of sustainable freight transport strategies?

RQ 4.1: Which success factors promote the implementation of PI networks?

RQ 4.2: Which policy measures promote the implementation of multimodal transport?

RQ 4.3: Which policy measures promote the implementation of LNG as an alternative fuel?

Again, the three sub research questions are answered in the three papers which constitute this thesis. Plasch *et al.* (2021) [Paper I] elaborate success factors for horizontal collaboration in a PI network. Success factors represent requirements needed to collaborate continuously in the PI network. If the success factors are not present, the partners will leave (or not even join) the PI network. Therefore, measures can be derived on how to establish the required success factors (RQ

3.1). Pfoser (in press) [Paper II] develops policy measures to facilitate multimodal freight transport (RQ 3.2). Pfoser *et al.* (2018d) [Paper III] present policy measures to promote LNG as an alternative fuel (RQ 3.3). In the present manuscript, the results of the sub research questions 3.1 – 3.3 are merged to answer the overarching RQ 3 and summarize the policy measures for sustainable freight transport acceptance.

1.4   Outline

The remainder of this thesis is organized as follows: Chapter 2 gives the conceptual background for this thesis. It will be defined what acceptance means in the context of sustainable freight transport. Furthermore, the prevalent typology to classify policy measures for sustainable freight transport is presented. Chapter 3 describes the research design of this thesis. Chapter 4 introduces the ASI (avoid-shift-improve) framework and gives an overview of existing strategies for sustainable freight transport. In particular, the three strategies chosen as subject of this thesis (PI, multimodality, LNG) will be presented and differentiated from similar concepts. It will be justified why these three particular strategies have been chosen as subject of this thesis.

Chapter 5 discusses the acceptance of sustainable freight transport strategies. First, the theoretical foundation of sustainable freight transport acceptance will be given. Finally, the acceptance of horizontal collaboration in a PI network, the acceptance of multimodal freight transport, and the acceptance of LNG as an alternative fuel are compared and the overarching determinants for the acceptance of sustainable freight transport are derived.

Chapter 6 presents policy measures to promote sustainable freight transport. First, a theoretical framework is developed to support the development of policy measures. This is followed by an overview of market failures in the sustainable freight transport market to point out which problems have to be addressed by the policy measures. Finally, policy measures for horizontal collaboration in a PI network, multimodal freight transport, and for LNG as an alternative fuel are compared and overarching policy measures to promote the acceptance of sustainable freight transport are suggested.

The concluding Chapter 7 closes this thesis with a synthesis of results, responses to the research questions, a presentation of the contributions to the domain of sustainable freight transport and a short outlook with some suggestions for future research.

Conceptual Background 2

2.1 Definition of the Term Acceptance

Existing literature offers a myriad of different definitions and classifications of the concept of acceptance. The ambiguous use of the term acceptance is problematic since a clear definition is needed before it can be evaluated and understood how acceptance is formed (Adell *et al.*, 2018). If there exists no clear definition, there is a severe risk of misinterpretation and misjudgment of research results concerning users' acceptance. This subchapter is therefore dedicated to the definition of the term acceptance.

Studying the acceptance of a target group is an important task because acceptance is a critical success factor for the realization of innovations (Geldmacher *et al.*, 2017). Acceptance constitutes "a psychological process that starts with pure interest in an innovation and leads toward the (regular) use of this innovation" (Geldmacher *et al.*, 2017, p. 272). Notably, the actual start and end of the acceptance process depend heavily on the specific definition. Several definitions refer to different stages of acceptance: some definitions require system use as a result of acceptance, others only refer to a positive attitude as the end of the acceptance process. Due to this variety of nuances, the different stages of acceptance will be discussed in the following.

2.1.1 Stages of Acceptance

Existing definitions on acceptance vary considerably regarding the degree of commitment required for the specific innovation under study. Different stages of acceptance can be identified ranging from stages with low commitment required

© The Author(s) 2022
S. Pfoser, *Decarbonizing Freight Transport*,
https://doi.org/10.1007/978-3-658-37103-6_2

to characterize acceptance (e.g. usefulness) to stages where high commitment is
required to characterize acceptance (actual system use). Figure 2.1 illustrates the
different stages of acceptance, which are related to the constructs of the technology acceptance model (usefulness, attitude, intention to use and actual system
use; to be later discussed in subchapter 5.1.3).

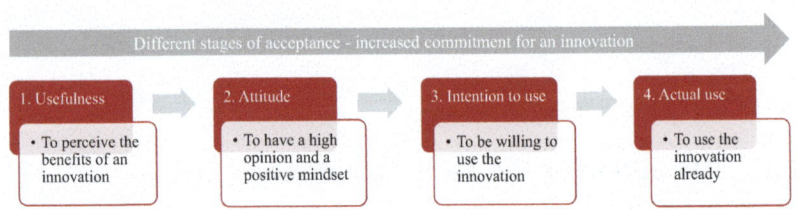

Figure 2.1 Stages of acceptance

Defining acceptance by the usefulness
The most elementary stage of acceptance is usefulness, i.e. the benefits or gain that
users expect to obtain by adopting an innovation. Some authors refer to usefulness
to define acceptance, as they claim that users accept a system or a technology when
they find it useful. For example, Nielsen (1993, p. 24) states that acceptance is
"basically the question whether the system is good enough to satisfy all the needs
and requirements of the users and other potential stakeholders". An example for
this first acceptance stage would be if an organization (or its transport manager)
considers alternative fuels as useful to reduce their carbon footprint. However, this
explanation of acceptance falls very short as considering a system as useful does
not imply that an individual would actually use this system.

Defining acceptance by the attitude
The next stage of acceptance involves having a positive attitude about an innovation. Attitude can be described as "a psychological tendency that is expressed by
evaluating a particular entity with some degree of favor or disfavor" (Eagly and
Chaiken, 1993, p. 1). Some authors state that having a positive opinion and mindset
towards a system or technology implies that the system/technology is accepted. For
example, Risser and Lehner (1998, p. 8) describe that "acceptance refers to what
the objects or contents for which acceptance is measured are associated to; what do
those objects or contents imply for the asked person". Compared to the first stage
of acceptance which is bound up with rational considerations about the usability of
an innovation, this second stage of acceptance is additionally driven by the users'

emotions towards the innovation, which are reflected in their attitude (Adell *et al.*, 2018). This second stage of acceptance is also referred to as *attitudinal acceptance* (Ausserer and Risser, 2005). Attitudinal acceptance is a consequence of considering the usefulness of an innovation. An example for attitudinal acceptance would be if an organization appreciates alternative fuels as effective and viable option to reduce their carbon footprint, but they think they do not need alternative fuels for their company. Therefore, the second acceptance stage is still not related to the use of an innovation (Ausserer and Risser, 2005).

Defining acceptance by the intention to use
The third stage of acceptance is related to the will to use an innovation or a technology, which is also called the intention to use. Some authors equate acceptance with intention to use, for example Chismar and Wiley-Patton (2003). The intention to use can either rest on practical experience of the system or on theoretical knowledge and judgment (Adell *et al.*, 2018). The latter is also known as *"a priori acceptance"*, i.e. the evaluation of a system or technology before having actual contact to the system/technology (Payre *et al.*, 2014). The intention to use an innovation is a consequence of attitudinal acceptance. An example for this acceptance stage would be if an organization is willing to use alternative fuels though they are not using them at currently (and possibly have no experience with alternative fuels).

Defining acceptance by the actual system use
The last stage of acceptance involves full commitment to an innovation, as the innovation is already in practical use at this stage. Several authors stipulate that acceptance only occurs in combination with actual system use, for example Dillon and Morris (1996) state that acceptance must be demonstrable by the employment of the technology under study. This type of acceptance is also referred to as *behavioral acceptance*, because acceptance is expressed by actual behaviour (Schmalfuß *et al.*, 2017). Actual system use is a consequence of the intention to use an innovation. An example for this last acceptance stage would be if an organization actually uses alternative fuels.

2.1.2 Further Differentiation of Acceptance

Beside the above described classification of acceptance stages, there are some further ways to differentiate various types of acceptance. To better grasp the concept of acceptance, some common differentiations that frequently occur in the literature will be discussed in the following.

The classification of *attitudinal and behavioral acceptance* has already been introduced above: attitudinal acceptance is based on the opinion and emotion regarding the innovation, while behavioral acceptance is based on observable behavior such as actual system use (Sadvandi and Halkias, 2019). Attitudinal and behavioral acceptance related to transport (e.g. intelligent transport systems or automated driving) is for example differentiated in Ausserer and Risser (2005), Schmalfuß *et al.* (2017), Xu *et al.* (2018) or Sadvandi and Halkias (2019).

Another type of acceptance frequently mentioned in the literature is *conditional acceptance*. Conditional acceptance suggests that acceptance depends upon specific conditions or requirements. Ziefle *et al.* (2015) evaluate the conditional acceptance of electric mobility in public transport and find that safety and security issues are a precondition for acceptance. Conditional acceptance in context of transport can be found in Grisolía and López del Pino (2008) or Ziefle *et al.* (2015).

Similar to conditional acceptance, *contextual acceptance* refers to acceptance which depends on situational factors and the context (Adell *et al.*, 2018). Saad (2004) states that situational context plays an important role to induce behavioral change. An example for contextual acceptance would be if multimodal freight transport is accepted for regular transport services, but not in the context of time-critical express deliveries.

The concept of a *priori acceptance* has already been explained above: it is the acceptance without any practical experience of the technology or system. Payre *et al.* (2014), Brookhuis *et al.* (2019) and Kaye *et al.* (2020) study the a priori acceptance of automated cars and driver assistance systems. The counterpart of a priori acceptance is *a posteriori acceptance*, which means acceptance after having tried a technology or system (Adell *et al.*, 2018). Schmid and Graf (2016) suggest that a priori and a posteriori acceptance of a navigation display for aviation are diverging.

2.1.3 Defining Acceptance in Context of Sustainable Freight Transport

As illustrated in the preceding Subchapters 2.1.1 and 2.1.2, there are manifold ways to define and view acceptance. Common to all of the above described definitions is that the user (either potential or factual) of a system or technology makes a judgement about the system or technology. To specify how the concept of acceptance is understood in this thesis, a definition of acceptance in context of sustainable freight transport will be given now. Based on the considerations of different types of acceptance elaborated above, the following definition of acceptance is proposed for this thesis:

Acceptance is the extent to which an organization is willing to implement a sustainable freight transport strategy and, when available, to incorporate the strategy in the logistics companies' transport operations.

This definition accounts for several key aspects of acceptance, which ensures that acceptance is a functional construct when developing and promoting sustainable transport strategies. First of all, the definition stresses a *user-centric* view, as logistics companies are the users of sustainable transport strategies, i.e. they are those players that realize sustainable freight transport. It is the logistics companies' *perception and understanding* of sustainable transport strategies which is relevant for the implementation of these strategies, and not the actual effects that are bound up with the strategies (Schade and Baum, 2007). For example, if logistics companies do not perceive it beneficial to collaborate in a PI network, then the PI will fail, although it is proven by pilot studies (e.g. Sarraj *et al.*, 2014) that there are benefits. It is also important to view the benefits from the logistics companies' perspective, since the organizational perspective often deviates from the societal/political perspective (Adell *et al.*, 2018). For example, organizations value profitability very high, while the societal/political perspective also emphasizes the ecological benefits.

By referring to "the *extent* of acceptance", this definition acknowledges that the different stages of acceptance as described above exist. It thereby reflects the continuous nature of the construct acceptance. For a low-carbon freight transport system it is important that sustainable strategies are realized in practice, which emphasizes those stages of acceptance which are related to behavioral changes, namely intention to use and actual system use (Adell *et al.*, 2018). Due to the fact that sustainable transport strategies can only bring positive effects when they are actually used, the definition focuses on the latter two acceptance stages (intention to use and actual system use). Xu *et al.* (2018) argue that the determinants of attitudinal acceptance are not necessarily the same as the determinants for actual use of a technology. Attitudinal acceptance does not materialize the actual uptake of an innovation and is therefore not targeted by the definition.

2.2   Definition and Classification of Policy Measures

Policy measures are instruments used by governmental authorities to effect or prevent a particular societal change (Vedung, 2010). In context of this thesis, the desired societal change is the implementation of sustainable transport strategies in the logistics industry. Policy measures to promote sustainable freight transport belong to the wide group of environmental policy instruments. Environmental policy instruments have been previously defined as "the set of techniques by which governmental authorities wield their power in attempting to affect society- in terms of values and beliefs, action and organization- in such a way as to improve, or to prevent the deterioration of, the quality of the natural environment" (Mickwitz, 2003, p. 419). This definition is useful to explain policy measures for sustainable freight transport. Hence, it can be substantiated that policy measures for sustainable freight transport aim to affect logistics companies in terms of values and beliefs, action and organization, such that the negative environmental impact of freight transport is mitigated.

A plethora of different policy measures exists, likewise there are a variety of classification schemes (Vedung, 2010). Essentially, policy measures can be classified according to the level of intervention, i.e. the degree of authoritative force they involve (Weber *et al.*, 2014). Figure 2.2 shows that there is a difference between hard policy measures and soft policy measures. The former are mandatory and quite restrictive, as they force a specific behavior (high intervention level), while the latter are less restrictive and rely on voluntary behavioral change (low intervention level). Policy instrument theories typically refer to three main types of measures, namely regulation ("sticks"), economic incentives ("carrots") and information instruments ("sermons") (Bax, 2011).

An alternative approach is to differentiate between technology push instruments and market-pull instruments (Vollenbroek, 2002; Horbach *et al.*, 2012). Technology-push measures promote technological advancement, for example by research and development programs. Market-Pull measures aim to increase the demand for sustainable innovations, e.g. through awareness campaigns or eco-labelling (Al-Saleh and Mahroum, 2015). The technology-push and market-pull typology has, however, been criticized as both push and pull rely heavily on subsidization and are not necessarily sustainably efficient (Taylor, 2008). Hereafter, the popular typology of sticks, carrots and sermons (Figure 2.2) will be used to discuss the variety of potential policy measures. Each measure will be presented in detail in the following subsections.

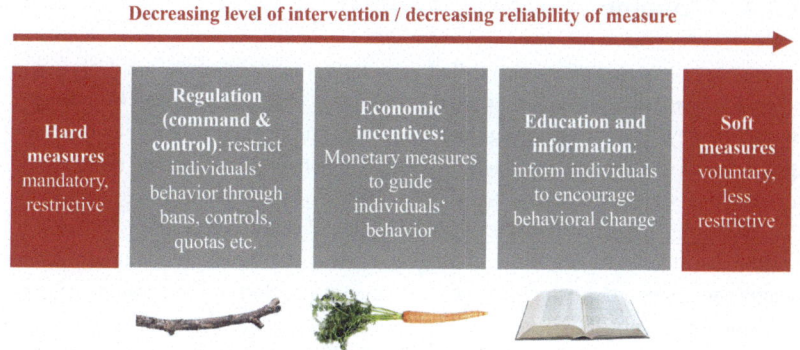

Figure 2.2 Classification of policy measures

2.2.1 Regulation (Sticks)

Regulations limit users' opportunities to follow a specific behavior, e.g. by setting standards, technology controls, bans or permits or by introducing zoning and other input restrictions or output quotas (Mickwitz, 2003; Perman *et al.*, 2003). Regulations may be derived from official legislative acts, such as directives, but they may be also derived from so-called "soft law" such as action plans, policy targets, guidelines and other policy documents (Bax, 2011). Regulation measures are mandatory by nature as they imply rules of conduct and prescribe a particular behavior. Thereby, they are also referred to as "command and control". The advantage of regulations is that they allow governmental authorities to enforce the desired behavior by law, thus there is high confidence about the target groups' compliance with the restrictions (Taylor *et al.*, 2012). Monitoring and enforcing the compliance may however be costly and onerous, therefore regulations are typically part of a policy mix which includes other instruments as well (Simeonova and Diaz-Bone, 2005). Regulations often involve negative connotations, as they are associated with threats of unfavorable sanctions such as punishments, fines, etc. (Vedung, 2010). Despite that, setting regulations is quite a frequently used intervention option in many industrialized regions (Mickwitz, 2003).

2.2.2 Economic Incentives (Carrots)

Economic policy measures, also called monetary policy measures, are designed to promote the market uptake of a particular behavior. This may happen by influencing the money, time or effort that has to be spent to pursue this behavior (Vedung, 2010). Economic incentives make a particular behavior cheaper or more costly for the involved market players. A major difference compared to regulations is that the target group is not forced to adopt the desired behavior in the case of economic / monetary incentives. Instead, there is still the freedom to choose whether to change the behavior or not (Perman *et al.*, 2003). For example, if governments offer subsidies for companies, the companies are not obliged to claim these subsidies, they can decide independently if the subsidy is worth changing a particular behavior or taking a particular action desired by the government. Monetary disincentives function in a similar manner (Vedung, 2010). For example, if governments raise a tax to prevent a particular behavior, they do not prohibit this behavior, they simply make the behavior more expensive and thus still leave the freedom to choose up to the market players. An alternative type of economic incentive is to create a market for environmental resources, e.g. through tradable emissions certificates or through the introduction of resource quotas (Opschoor, 1994).

Economic incentives are known to be more cost-effective than command and control measures, however it is less predictable whether economic incentives will suffice since it is uncertain whether the addressed target group will react to the market measures provided (Gunningham and Sinclair, 1999). Economic incentives can also have unintended side effects, for example distributional effects which negatively affect the poor or distortions pushing up prices (Taylor *et al.*, 2012).

2.2.3 Information (Sermons)

Education and information measures aim for knowledge transfer to persuade target groups to change their behavior. They are therefore also called "suasive policy measures" (Mickwitz, 2003). Different means of communication are available to inform about current problems, possible solutions and actions required to tackle these problems, as well as reasoned arguments to convince the target group to adopt the desired behavior. Among the diverse set of communication options there are printed materials (flyers, booklets, brochures, etc.), training programs (courses, lecture series, information talks, etc.) or demonstration programs

(Vedung, 2010). All these instruments are suitable to inform about recommended actions and behavior suggested to achieve a policy goal. Information measures also include instruments where the public authority authorizes private actors to distribute environmental information. This is the case with eco-labelling or environmental management systems, which are also suitable to convince market players of sustainable behavior (Mickwitz, 2003).

Similar to the economic incentives, no mandatory obligation results from education and information instruments- target groups still have the freedom to choose whether they follow the behavior advised according to the education measures (Vedung, 2010). A main difference compared to economic incentives is that no resources are given to or taken from the target groups to influence their behavior. Information and education measures are therefore relatively non-intrusive and non-coercive in nature (Gunningham and Sinclair, 1999) and constitute the least restrictive type of policy measures. At the same time, information measures are the instrument with the lowest reliability, because they are based on voluntariness and awareness of the target group (Taylor *et al.*, 2012). Despite that, the use of information measures has recently gained popularity in Europe as it is regarded a contemporary way to elicit the desired behavior simply by allowing for an improved understanding of the consequences of the target groups' actions (Bax, 2011).

Research Design

3

3.1 Methodology and Data Collection

In this thesis, the cases of three different sustainable freight transport strategies are studied to be able to compare the acceptance of these strategies and evaluate if there are any patterns among them. As illustrated above, these three strategies are horizontal collaboration in a PI network, multimodal freight transport and LNG as an alternative fuel. This approach makes it possible to derive overarching determinants of sustainable freight transport acceptance and general policy measures which are suitable to promote sustainable freight transport. A rich data set was collected for all three cases to provide empirical evidence for this thesis. For collecting this data, a mixture of qualitative and quantitative research methods were used (Table 3.1), though the main focus was on qualitative methods (in-depth interviews, focus groups) due to the explorative nature of the research objectives. Figure 3.1 gives an overview of the empirical work conducted in the course of this thesis.

The data set was collected within the framework of several large research projects in which the author took part. These research projects are:

- *ATROPINE*—Fast track to the Physical Internet, funded by the State of Upper Austria in order to design a 'Physical Internet Innovation Chain' for the economic region of Upper Austria. The duration of this project was from December 2015 to May 2018.
- *ChemMultimodal*—Promotion of multimodal transport in the chemical industry, funded by Interreg Central Europe in order to increase the share of multimodal transport in the chemical goods industry. The duration of this project was from June 2016 to May 2019.

© The Author(s) 2022
S. Pfoser, *Decarbonizing Freight Transport*,
https://doi.org/10.1007/978-3-658-37103-6_3

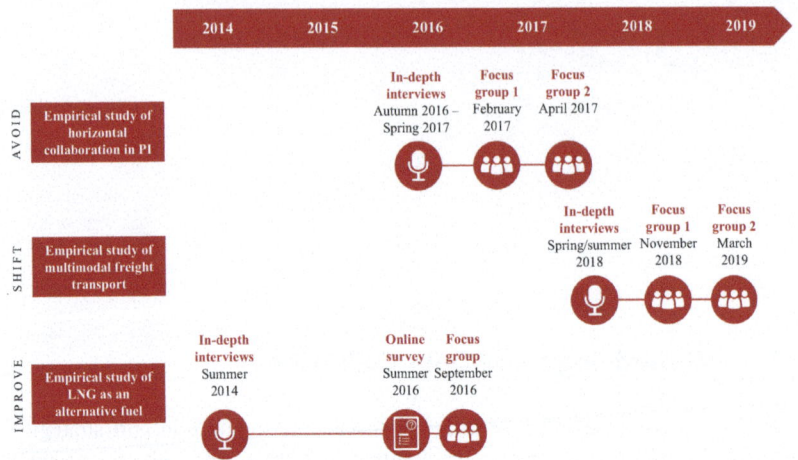

Figure 3.1 Procedure and time frame of empirical work

- *LNG Masterplan for Rhine-Main-Danube*—funded by the European TEN-T programme to facilitate the implementation of LNG as an alternative fuel in line with the EU transport, energy and environmental policy goals. The duration of this project was from January 2013 to December 2015.
- *LiquID*—Identifying the market potential of LNG in Austria, funded by the Austrian Ministry of Transport to assess the feasibility of introducing LNG as an alternative fuel in Austria. The duration of this project was from October 2015 to September 2016.

All four research projects are characterized by an intense involvement of the relevant stakeholders. The projects aimed to promote the specific sustainable transport strategy, be it the PI, multimodality or LNG, and therefore the main target group(s) of these strategies are addressed in the study. Table 3.1 shows which stakeholders were involved in which case study. The intense target group involvement fits with the "demand perspective" described in subchapter 1.2, which is currently neglected in sustainable freight transport studies. It is well known that whether an innovation will be accepted or rejected by its target group depends heavily on the way that user needs are integrated in the development of this innovation (Ausserer and Risser, 2005). It is recommended to involve users as early as possible in the development process to ensure their acceptance of new innovations such as sustainable freight transport strategies. This is why the target groups are deeply involved in the projects. The aim is to obtain user-centric measures which fit the needs of the target group and thereby encourage the implementation of sustainable freight transport. But who are the target groups of the sustainable freight transport strategies under study in this thesis? Three main parties in freight transport come into question (Figure 3.2). First, there are *transport providers*, who supply the required infrastructure (e.g. multimodal terminals or refueling stations). Logistics companies, e.g. logistics service providers (LSPs) are the *transport users*, because they operate transport services in their daily business. And finally, *transport customers* consume the transport services offered by the logistics companies. Shippers such as manufacturers and other industrial companies belong to the group of transport customers.

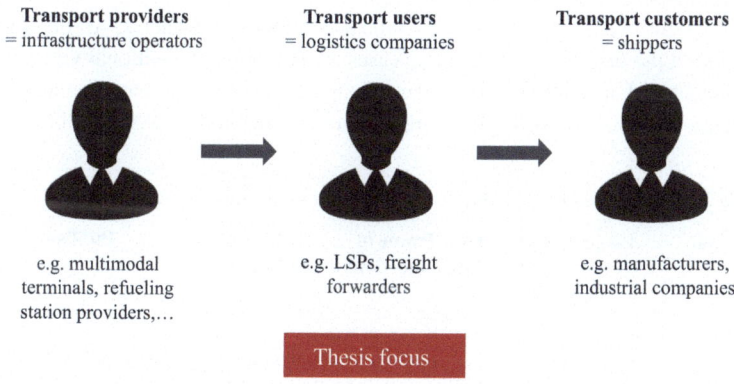

Figure 3.2 Main freight transport parties

Logistics companies are the party which realizes freight transport and in this regard they have the authority to implement sustainable practices. Transport providers are the ones that enable sustainable freight transport by supplying the required infrastructure. Transport customers are the ones that may request sustainable practices from their LSP. But in the end, the logistics company is the party which has the competence (and opportunity) to enforce sustainable freight transport (Martinsen, 2014). The logistics company has to share its resources in a PI network, and the logistics company has to operate LNG trucks. Therefore, it can be expected that logistics companies are affected the most by sustainable freight transport strategies. The focus of this thesis is therefore on logistics companies as the "users" of the transport system, and the intention is to develop user-centric policy measures which meet logistics companies' requirements and promote their acceptance of sustainable freight transport. The three cases involve a number of Austrian logistics companies and bring in their perspectives on the PI, multimodality and LNG. The logistics companies are either involved as interview partners, focus group participants, or survey respondents. Additionally, some of them provided archival data about their business (Table 3.1).

Beside the undisputed importance of logistics companies, other stakeholders are relevant as well. For that reason, other parties are involved in the empirical investigations. As mentioned above, infrastructure providers supply the required facilities for sustainable freight transport. Shippers influence transport services with their requests. Other stakeholder groups are also relevant, as they know the market mechanisms of sustainable freight transport very well, e.g. research and development (R&D) institutions or regional development agencies. All these parties enrich the discussion of the three cases as they provide additional viewpoints and insights. Especially for the focus groups it was vital to have multifaceted discussions about the topic, therefore additional stakeholders were involved.

Table 3.1 Overview of methods and materials used in this thesis

Method	Target group (respondents/ participants)	Time frame of data collection	Output (data collected)	Published in
PI case study				
In-depth interviews	Three LSPs and four shippers	Autumn 2016 – spring 2017	17 semi-structured interviews, each recorded and transcribed	Plasch *et al.* (2021)
Focus groups	Three LSPs and four shippers	February 2017 and April 2017	Two focus groups with more than 40 participants. Detailed protocols and meeting notes	Plasch *et al.* (2021)
Archival data	Seven shippers/LSPs	Autumn 2016 – spring 2017	Data about transport routes, warehouse utilization and shipment demands for one fiscal year	Plasch *et al.* (2021)

(continued)

Table 3.1 (continued)

Method	Target group (respondents/ participants)	Time frame of data collection	Output (data collected)	Published in
Multimodality case study				
In-depth interviews	Ten LSPs	Spring/summer 2018	Ten semi-structured interviews, each recorded and transcribed	Pfoser (in press)
Focus groups	Ten LSPs + infrastructure providers, shippers, regional development agencies and R&D	November 2018 and March 2019	Two focus groups with more than 30 participants. Detailed protocols and meeting notes	Pfoser (in press)
Archival data	Three shippers/LSPs	Spring/summer 2018	Data about transport routes and shipment demands	Pfoser (in press)
LNG case study				
In-depth interviews	Six LSPs + nine other HGV fleet operators	Summer 2014	15 semi-structured interviews, detailed notes and protocols	Pfoser et al. (2016)
Online survey	Stakeholders along the LNG value chain	Summer 2016	Filled questionnaires (157 responses)	Pfoser *et al.* (2018d)
Focus group	Stakeholders along the LNG value chain	September 2016	Focus group with 18 participants. Detailed protocol and meeting notes	Pfoser *et al.* (2018d)

3.2 Theoretical Perspectives

The research process in this thesis also comprises the development of a theoretical framework to establish the theoretical background of the underlying two research objectives. The theoretical background is twofold (Figure 3.3). On the one hand, the acceptance of sustainable freight transport strategies (research objective 1 of this thesis) is explained. For that purpose, behavioral theories are used to describe logistics companies' acceptance (Subchapter 5.1). On the other hand, theoretical support for the development of policy measures is given (research objective 2 of this thesis). A number of organizational theories are used to derive implications on how to set policy measures which encourage logistics companies to implement sustainable practices (Subchapter 6.1).

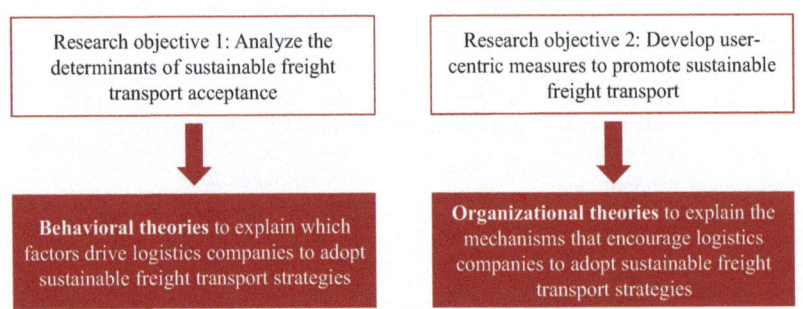

Figure 3.3 Theoretical perspectives in the thesis

Strategies for Sustainable Freight Transport

4

4.1 Avoid-Shift-Improve (ASI) Framework

The most prominent and frequently quoted definition of sustainability is published in the Brundtland Report, where it is written that "sustainable development is development that meets the needs of the present without compromising the ability of future generations to meet their needs" (World Commission on Environment and Development, 1987, p. 8). According to Daly (1990), there are three main operational guidelines that should be followed to ensure sustainable development, namely:

- Renewable resources should not be used faster than their regeneration rates.
- Non-renewable resources should not be used faster than substitutes become available.
- Pollution emissions should not exceed the assimilative capacity of the environment.

It is well known that the transportation sector extensively contravenes all of these three guidelines (McKinnon et al., 2015; Szyliowicz, 2003). Transport contributes a quarter of total greenhouse gas emissions in the EU-28, most of which comes from road transport (Figure 4.1). Nearly three quarters of the total transport GHG emissions stems from road transport, followed by aviation (13.9%) and maritime transport (13.3%). The share of emissions from railways and other transport modes (inland waterway transport, pipelines,...) amounts to 1% and are therefore negligible (European Environment Agency, 2019b).

© The Author(s) 2022
S. Pfoser, *Decarbonizing Freight Transport*,
https://doi.org/10.1007/978-3-658-37103-6_4

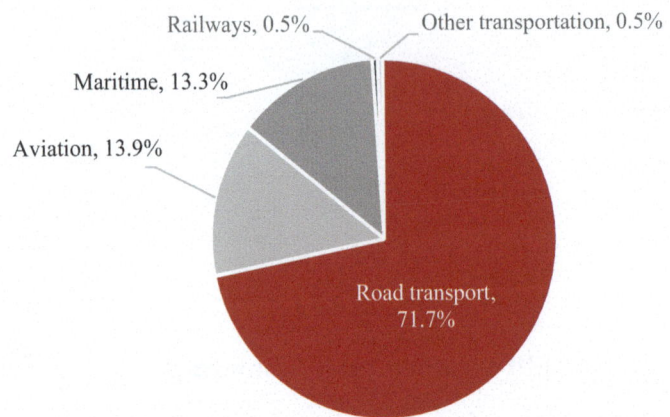

Figure 4.1 Share of European transport GHG emissions by transport mode. (data from European Environment Agency, 2019b)

Figure 4.1 clearly underlines that strategies have to be implemented to mitigate the environmental impact of road transport. The avoid-shift-improve (ASI) approach is a well-known framework to summarize the three main strategies that exist to reduce GHG emissions from transport in general, and from road transport in particular (Bongardt *et al.*, 2019). These three main strategies constitute the three pillars of ASI (Dalkmann and Brannigan, 2014):

(1) *Avoid or reduce transport:* Aims to improve the overall efficiency of the transport system as a whole by implementing strategies that reduce the number of shipments or trip length.
(2) *Shift transport:* Aims to improve individual shipment efficiency by promoting a modal shift from the most energy consuming transport mode (road) towards low-carbon transport modes (railways, waterways).
(3) *Improve transport:* Aims to improve the energy efficiency of transport modes and related vehicle technology, e.g. by using low-carbon fuels and increasing fuel efficiency.

The ASI approach is focused on demand side measures for sustainable transport and offers a holistic framework for an overall optimization of the transport system regarding sustainability aspects (Bongardt *et al.*, 2019). The initial development of the ASI approach dates back to the early 1990s in Germany, where ASI was established to structure policy measures for sustainable transport (Bongardt *et al.*, 2019). ASI was first mentioned in 1994 in a report by the German parliament´s Enquete Commission (Deutscher Bundestag, 1994). There is a hierarchy among the three pillars of the ASI approach which should be observed when implementing sustainable transport measures: Avoid strategies should be of first priority as they have the highest potential to reduce the environmental impact of freight transport. However, avoid strategies are challenging to implement as they are bound up with renunciation and abandonment (Mauch *et al.*, 2001). Next, shift strategies should be implemented; and finally, when the other two strategies are fully exhausted, improve strategies should be realized (Kagermeier, 1998). The ASI approach is a universal framework into which a large range of diverse policies, regulatory instruments and best practices fit. ASI does not stipulate the scope of the measures- gradual and incremental changes are covered as well as radical paradigm shifts (Bakker *et al.*, 2014). There is increasing attention on the ASI framework. A number of international NGOs and development organizations have already dedicated themselves to the ASI approach, not only in Europe, but also on other continents like Asia or Latin America (Huizenga and Leather, 2012). The International Energy Agency also refers to the ASI approach in their scenarios depicting the GHG emissions mitigation potential of the transport sector to reach the 2° C limit of global warming by 2050 (Fulton *et al.*, 2013).

In the following subchapters, the three pillars of ASI will be investigated further. For each pillar, one strategy to implement this pillar will be introduced in detail, namely:

- Horizontal collaboration and bundling in a PI network (AVOID)
- Multimodality (SHIFT)
- LNG as an alternative fuel (IMPROVE).

The state-of-the-art knowledge on these strategies will be presented and it will be justified why these three strategies have been chosen to represent the respective ASI pillar.

4.2 Avoid Transport—PI Collaboration & Bundling

Heavy goods vehicles are estimated to run empty 30% of the time in Europe (Freight Transport Association, 2019). Before considering how to increase the efficiency of freight transport by modal shift or technological improvements, it should therefore be carefully appraised whether it is possible to avoid or reduce transport activities to avert empty trucks. Avoiding transport is the most effective, but also the most difficult strategy to achieve more sustainable transport. For the sustained reduction of freight transport, a paradigm shift will be necessary to change the habits and behavior of transport stakeholders (McKinnon, 2018; Wittenbrink, 2015). The formation of collaborative relationships is a key strategy to avoid transport by bundling transport streams and increasing the utilization of transport assets (Bretzke, 2014). Partnerships between different organizations in the logistics chain are seen as a promising solution to overcome the problem of increasing freight volumes in future (Punte *et al.*, 2019; Wittenbrink, 2015; Bretzke, 2014). Based on the level of interaction among organizations involved in the partnership it is distinguished between *coordination, cooperation* and *collaboration* (Kotzab *et al.*, 2018). Coordination denotes the lowest level of interaction where single activities are harmonized or synchronized between organizations. Cooperation means working together as equal partners, whereas collaboration calls for organizations to act as one single entity (Kotzab *et al.*, 2018).

Collaboration in the context of logistics and supply chain management dates back to the mid-1990s when the strategy of collaborative planning forecasting and replenishment became popular (Barratt, 2004). Horizontal logistics collaboration is a particular type of partnership that involves active collaboration between two or more organizations that operate on the same level of the supply chain and perform comparable logistics services (Pomponi *et al.*, 2015). Mason *et al.* (2007) stated that horizontal transport collaboration comes along with various synergies such as cost minimization, value creation, improved service levels or increased end customer satisfaction. There exist several requirements to realize these synergies, including trust among partners, common suppliers and delivery bases, a capable orchestrator and an effective business model, including a fair gain sharing system (Sanchez Rodrigues *et al.*, 2015; Cruijssen *et al.*, 2007). Horizontal collaboration constitutes a megatrend in transport and logistics that is predicted to influence the logistics industry tremendously during the coming decades (Grazia Speranza, 2018; Stank *et al.*, 2015).

In past, several types of collaboration models evolved in logistics each of which has distinct characteristics and operating principles (Figure 4.2). A myriad of different names were attached to these collaboration models, including transport marketplaces, alliances, coalitions, logistics pooling, synchromodality or the Physical Internet, to name just a few (Pan *et al.*, 2019).

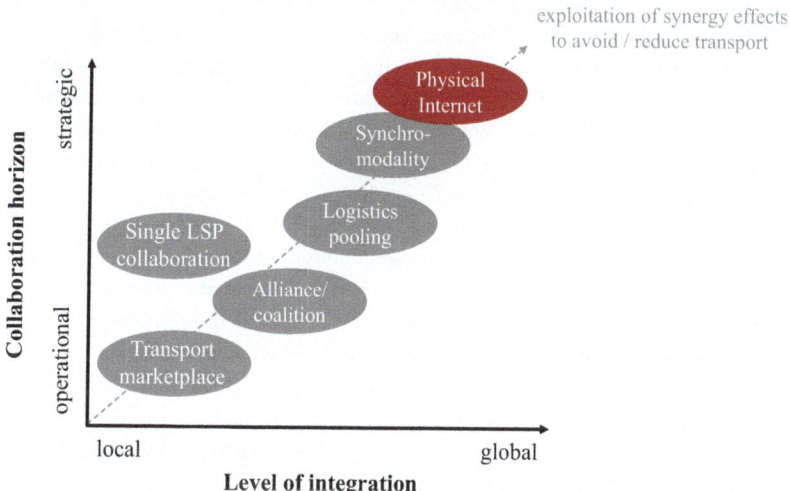

Figure 4.2 Comparison of collaboration models in logistics

The Physical Internet (PI) is a recently emerging logistics concept which can be considered as the most advanced collaboration model currently existing in transport and logistics (Figure 4.2). The PI is a vision which uses today's interdependent IT networks and the digital internet environment as a role model to reorganize freight transport (Montreuil, 2011; Montreuil *et al.*, 2013). Collaboration plays a central role in the idea of the PI. PI involves horizontal collaboration among logistics service providers and also among shippers to reduce the environmental impact of their freight transport activities (Ambra *et al.*, 2019).

Compared to the other concepts presented in Figure 4.2, the PI is progressive. The PI tries to utilize the advantages of several collaboration models by minimizing their disadvantages. For example, partnerships in the PI aim for global long-term relations, as opposed to *transport marketplaces*, where short-term, operational transactions take place only to perform single transport requests between individual partners (Caplice, 2007). Long-term collaboration is desirable because it involves mutual trust, increased commitment and higher reliability compared to short-term relationships (Humphries and Wilding, 2004). However, transport marketplaces are designed for cooperation at a temporary, operational level and they are mostly based on bilateral peer-to-peer agreements (Huang and Xu, 2013). *Single LSP collaborations* (or single carrier collaborations, Hernández *et al.*, 2011) also take place on a bilateral level as there are only two parties involved which collaborate with each other. However, compared to transport marketplaces, single LSP collaborations are entered for a longer period of time, and not only for single transport requests (Hernández *et al.*, 2011). The goals of single LSP collaborations from an LSPs' viewpoint are reduced transport costs, the acquisition of external capacities and improved customer services (Buijs *et al.*, 2016; Puettmann and Stadtler, 2010). Due to the bundling of transport requests, there will also be positive environmental effects resulting from single LSP collaboration.

An *alliance or coalition* between transport companies already promotes a more integrated and holistic view of freight transport as compared to transport marketplaces and single LSP collaborations (Pan *et al.*, 2019). In an alliance/coalition the collaboration is more stable and efficient, because it is no longer based on bilateral exchange, but on multilateral exchange (Pan *et al.*, 2019). The terms alliance and coalition are sometimes misused interchangeably, however, the difference is that an alliance is based on decentralized planning while a coalition is based on centralized planning (Dai and Chen, 2012; Li *et al.*, 2015).

Logistics pooling is an approach that is even more integrated than an alliance or coalition between transport companies. Logistics pooling is a collaboration model where vertical and horizontal collaboration are combined to exploit synergies between different supply chains (Mason *et al.*, 2007, Rodrigues *et al.*, 2015). Resources such as warehouses or transport resources are pooled and shared between the partners (Pan *et al.*, 2019). It is therefore quite a strategic and long-term type of collaboration model (Figure 4.2).

Synchromodality and the *Physical Internet* are the two most integrated and most strategic types of collaboration. Synchromodality and PI are interrelated to each other and reinforce each other (Ambra *et al.*, 2019). Both are quite new transport concepts that have been developed during the past ten years (Ambra *et al.*, 2019). Synchromodality and PI promote a holistic view of freight transport, including and combining all available transport capacities in a transport network in a highly flexible way (Montreuil, 2011; Behdani *et al.*, 2016). Compared with scheduling each transport request individually, the integrated network approach of synchromodality and PI provides a more efficient transportation plan resulting in a higher overall utilization of resources. An important principle which distinguishes synchromodality and PI from other logistics collaboration models is the fact that there is a central orchestrator, that means a neutral entity, which is allowed to modify transport constraints imposed by the shipper (van der Vorst *et al.*, 2016; Vanovermeire *et al.*, 2014). The central network orchestrator is sometimes also referred to as the "control tower" (Monios and Bergqvist, 2015). The central orchestrator has a holistic view of all transport demands and available resources in the network and is therefore able to consolidate freight flows, which leads to a better use of network capacities. (van Riessen *et al.*, 2015). In synchromodality, shippers book a-modal or mode-free transport services (Behdani *et al.*, 2016; Pfoser *et al.*, 2018a), which means that the shipper only determines basic framework conditions (delivery time, price cap) but not the transport mode. The a-modal booking allows the central orchestrator to make optimized decisions and real-time changes to the transportation plan (Guo *et al.*, 2017). Synchromodality is already a quite advanced type of collaboration (and could be a first step to realize PI), but PI is even more progressive. Unlike synchromodality, PI is additionally characterized by highly modularized, standardized and interoperable transport operations (Pan *et al.*, 2019). In PI, freight is moved in similar ways to data (packets) – smart, seamlessly within synchronized corridors and through hubs using the (open) networks of others (Lemmens *et al.*, 2019; Sáenz, 2016). Interoperability between all players involved in PI requires revolutionized planning, selection and pricing strategies in logistics networks with competitors collaborating (i.e. coopetition). The vision of PI also employs open and shared networks, using standard technical protocols, dynamic routing, deployment logics, control and optimizing intelligence and modular containers etc. (Montreuil, 2009).

The PI collaboration model was chosen as the focus of this thesis because it is the most advanced concept which entails the highest potential to exploit synergies between the collaborating partners. The implementation of the PI is also high on the political agenda in Europe. The technology platform ALICE includes the concept PI in their roadmap for logistics and supply chain management innovation (Zijm and Klumpp, 2016). ALICE anticipates a diverse number of benefits bound up with the full-fledged implementation of a PI network (Punte *et al.*, 2019; Steinberg and Norrman, 2017 Sarraj *et al.*, 2014; Montreuil, 2011):

- *Load consolidation*: Efficient pooling and cross-docking of loads from different suppliers and shippers. High capacity vehicles can be used for bigger load volumes and weights for longer distances. Pallets can be built from a mixture of different products, which allows for mixed load and weight volumes utilizing available space.
- *Asset sharing, open warehouses and transport networks*: Companies make use of the same vehicles (and other assets) to share idle capacities and increase asset utilization.

- *Back-hauling*: Empty returns can be avoided by picking up or delivering freight for collaborating partners on return trips.
- *Modular packaging and boxes*: collaborative re-design of transport packaging and containers to introduce modularity and optimal fit, allow efficient handling, consolidation and pooling.

Despite these numerous benefits, horizontal collaboration is challenging to achieve in the transport sector (Pfoser *et al.*, 2016b; van der Horst and Langen, 2008). Realizing the PI constitutes a paradigm shift in the current organization of transport and logistics (Ambra *et al.*, 2017). For the successful implementation of the PI it is necessary to know what influences the willingness to collaborate in a PI network, and how organizations can be encouraged to enter the PI network. These questions will be assessed in the subsequent Chapters 5 and 6.

4.3   Shift Transport—Multimodality

As illustrated in the introduction, the majority of freight transport is carried out by truck, and this is problematic because road transport causes a lot of negative externalities. Figure 4.3 compares the emission range of different transport modes. The numbers are based on default factors from the Global Logistics Emissions Council (GLEC) Framework, a globally recognized methodology for harmonized calculation and reporting of the logistics GHG footprint (Greene and Lewis, 2019). As can be seen in Figure 4.3, road transport and air transport produce much more emissions than any other transport mode. The emission ranges in Figure 4.3 represent well-to-wheel (WTW) emissions, which means that not only the environmental effects of burning the fuel in the vehicle are considered, but also the effects of producing and distributing the fuel are taken into account (Ramachandran and Stimming, 2015). The emission level of road freight transport depends on the type of vehicle that is used. Light-duty vehicles like vans or urban trucks cause far more emissions per ton kilometer than heavy goods vehicles (HGV). Anyway, the emissions of HGVs are still much higher than the emissions of inland waterways or railways. This illustrates the need for a modal shift away from roads to sustainable transport modes to reduce the environmental impact of logistics.

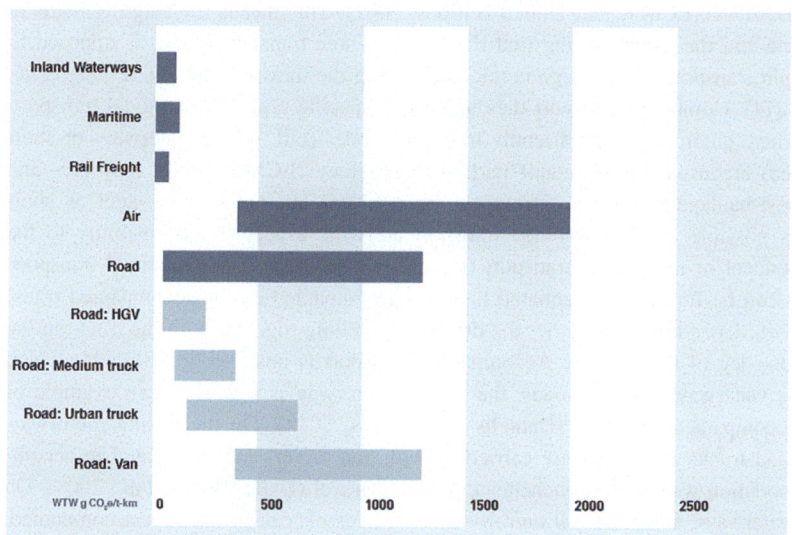

Figure 4.3 Indicative emission ranges for different types of freight transport. (Greene and Lewis, 2019)

The concept of multimodal freight transport (in short: multimodality) was already proposed four decades ago in order to shift cargo from road transport to sustainable transport modes. The original definition was set up by UNCTAD (1980) and characterizes multimodal transport as "the carriage of goods by at least two different modes of transport". Due to the combined use of multiple transport modes, the strengths of each mode can be utilized and the weaknesses can be compensated by the other mode(s). Thus, the cost effectiveness and sustainability of railway and waterways can be combined with the flexibility and speed of road transport (SteadieSeifi *et al.*, 2014).

Ever since the first definition of multimodality, a number of associated concepts arose which have to be distinguished carefully (Figure 4.4). These concepts include intermodal transport, combined transport, and co-modal transport. Out of all these transport concepts, multimodal transport is the most generic since it only requires the use of two or more modes of transport. Intermodal transport can be considered as a specific type of multimodal transport, "whereby two or more modes of transport are used to transport the same loading unit or truck in an integrated manner, without loading or unloading, in a [door to door] transport chain"

(UN/ECE, ECMT, EC, United Nations, 2001). This means the cargo remains in one and the same loading unit during the whole transport chain, as opposed to split transport where cargo is reloaded during the transport process (Posset *et al.*, 2014). Combined transport then again is a specific type of intermodal transport, where environmentally friendly transport modes (rail, inland waterways or short sea) are used for the major part of the journey (ECMT, 1998). Any pre- and post-haulage processes carried out by road are attempted to be kept as short as possible. Thus, combined transport adds the aspect of sustainability to the concept of intermodal transport (Reis, 2015). In respect of combined transport, it can be further differentiated between accompanied and unaccompanied transport, depending on whether the driver is travelling together with the truck on the long leg of the journey. Accompanied transport is possible on railroads as well as waterways. For railroads, the rolling motorway is a well-known example of accompanied transport (Danielis and Rotaris, 2014). On the rolling motorway, road trucks or trailers are carried by rail, and drivers may be seated in accommodation wagons or couchettes during rail travel (Dalla Chiara *et al.*, 2008). On waterways, so-called roll-on/roll-off (ro-ro) vessels can be used for accompanied, but also for unaccompanied transport. Road trucks, trailers or rail cars can be carried by ro-ro vessels (Fischer *et al.*, 2016). It is sometimes stated that multimodal transport solutions are only cost-efficient if they are carried out in an unaccompanied manner (López-Navarro *et al.*, 2011). In fact, the principal advantage of unaccompanied multimodal services is the reduction in personnel costs during the railborne / waterborne leg of the journey (Morales-Fusco *et al.*, 2018). However, the difficulty of unaccompanied shipments is the availability of drivers for the last mile of the transport chain, which will most probably be carried out on roads at the final freight destination.

In the further course of this thesis, the term multimodal transport will be used to denote the modal shift concepts presented in Figure 4.4, as multimodality serves as an umbrella term, which is often interchangeably used in the scientific literature and in practice. There is one more concept related to multimodality, which is not depicted in Figure 4.4, namely co-modal transport. Co-modality was defined by the European Commission in the midterm review of the White Paper on Transport (European Commission, 2006). The concept of co-modality strongly focuses on efficiency and the optimized use of transportation modes. It is defined as „the efficient use of different modes on their own and in combination" (European Commission, 2006, p. 4). Compared to the other transport concepts (multimodality, intermodality and combined transport), co-modality rather neglects the aspect of sustainability as unimodal road transport could also achieve the goal of co-modality, namely highest efficiency (Reis, 2015). A modal

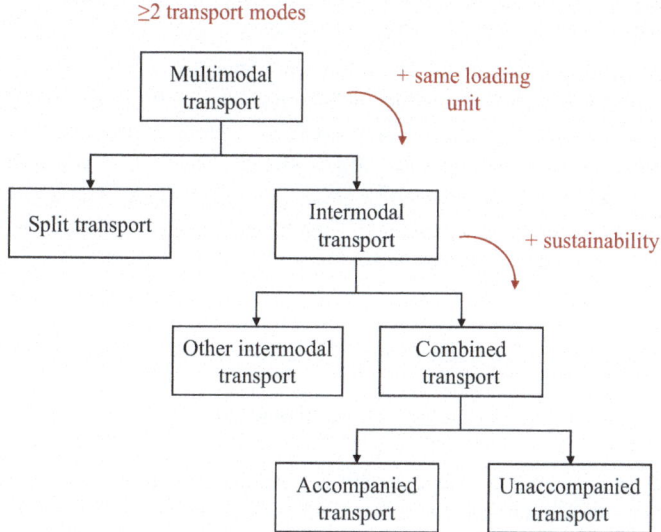

Figure 4.4 Classification of multimodal transport concepts. (based on Posset *et al.*, 2014 and Reis, 2015)

shift is therefore not inherent in co-modal transport. It should be noted that the term co-modality was mainly used by the European Commission and did not gain much practical importance. Co-modal transport is not within the scope of this thesis as sustainability is not a main goal of co-modal transport.

Although the idea of multimodal transport is already 40 years old, the relevance of this concept is still very high today. There exist strong political efforts to promote multimodal freight transport. For example, the European Commission has called for 2018 to be the "Year of Multimodality"—a year during which the Commission raised the importance of multimodality for the EU transport system in a series of activities (van Leijen, 2018). This commitment shows that European politics has strongly dedicated itself to multimodal freight transport as an effective way to improve the quality of life of European citizens, reduce air pollution and congestion, and reach the sustainability goals. Nevertheless, the share of sustainable transport modes is still very small compared to road transport in all European countries (European Commission, 2019). In 2014, the European Commission carried out a public consultation on multimodality and combined transport to get insights whether and how they should go on and promote these

modal shift concepts (European Commission, 2014). Responses were collected
from 18 EU member states and two non-member states, the respondents were
mainly business representatives. The results were unambiguously in favor of multimodal transport. The vast majority of the respondents (94%) claimed that the
European Commission should definitely continue to support multimodal transport
operations (European Commission, 2014). Otherwise they expect a reverse shift,
i.e. back from multimodal transport to unimodal road transport. The use of effective measures is therefore necessary to support the expansion and reinforcement
of multimodal freight operations in future.

4.4   Improve Transport—LNG as an Alternative Fuel

Improve strategies aim to increase the eco-efficiency of (mostly road) vehicles and
fleets (Mauch *et al.*, 2001). The increase in eco-efficiency is enabled by a number of clean technologies, for example low rolling-resistance tires, lightweight
design (e.g. aluminum wheels) or truck platooning (Punte *et al.*, 2019). Particular potential for eco-efficiency lies also in the development of alternative fuels
and propulsion systems. In the recent decades, several alternative fuel technologies have emerged including hydrogen, biofuels, electric and natural gas vehicles.
In the area of medium and heavy truck transport, natural gas is the alternative
which in the short-term is considered to be the best substitute for conventional
fuels since it comprises the potential to reduce environmental impacts and it is
readily available and accessible (Yeh, 2007). LNG, i.e. natural gas in its liquid
state, is the only alternative fuel which is well suited for heavy trucks of more
than 18 metric tons (Table 4.1).

Table 4.1 Application range of different alternative fuel technologies. (based on
Feldpausch-Jaegers *et al.*, 2016)

	Diesel	CNG	LNG	H2	Electric
Car (short distance)	++	++	--	+	++
Car (long distance)	++	++	--	+	+
Light truck (3.5 – 7.5 t)	++	++	-	+	+
Medium truck (7.5 – 18 t)	++	+	+	-	-
Heavy truck (>18 t)	++	+	++	--	--

++ fully applicable, + minor restrictions, - large restrictions, -- not applicable

The energy density of LNG is very high compared to other fuels. To convert natural gas to LNG, it has to be cooled down to a temperature of -162 °C where it becomes liquid and reduces its volume roughly 600 times (Arteconi et al., 2010). Due to this volume reduction, the energy density of LNG is much higher than, for example, of CNG (compressed natural gas), which is the reason why LNG can conveniently be used for heavy-duty and long distance transport, while CNG is rather used for passenger transport. The maximum driving range of LNG trucks is currently 1600 kilometers, while the maximum driving range of CNG vehicles is only 500 kilometers (Anderhofstadt and Spinler, 2019). The driving range of electric vehicles is even less, namely only up to 200 kilometers. This restricts the application areas of electric vehicles to urban logistics with short-distance transports and light vehicles (Anderhofstadt and Spinler, 2019). Further barriers for electric trucks consist in the high weight of battery packs which reduces the payload; and the recharging time, which is significantly longer and requires more energy for electric trucks than for electric cars (Engerer and Horn, 2010). Another type of alternative fuels is biofuel, e.g. bioethanol or biodiesel. Biofuels are gaseous or liquid fuels generated from biomass such as plant or animal waste (Kluschke et al., 2019). The main problem with biofuels is their limited availability which occurs because land use is primarily dedicated for food production (Duarte et al., 2014; Simio et al., 2013).

Due to the above described shortages of existing alternative fuel technologies, several truck manufacturers like Iveco and Scania currently focus on the development of LNG fueled trucks. Pioneering fleet owners have already started to purchase these LNG trucks. In summer 2018, the German Federal Ministry of Transport started a funding program to subsidize energy-efficient heavy-duty vehicles producing low CO_2 emissions. Statistics from October 2019 reveal that out of 1390 funding requests, 994 trucks were LNG-fueled, 339 trucks were CNG-fueled and only 57 trucks were electric (Völklein, 2019). Later on in February 2020, in total 1915 funding requests were submitted to the German Federal Ministry of Transport, out of which a high number of 1500 requests encompass LNG-fueled trucks, despite the fact that at that time the toll exemptions for LNG trucks were expected to expire at the end of 2019 (Landwehr, 2020).

In the long run, hydrogen is considered a highly promising alternative fuel technology by many experts (Table 4.2). Hydrogen trucks have an on-board hydrogen storage to generate electricity within a fuel cell (Kluschke et al., 2019). Prospects for the introduction of hydrogen as a transport fuel already started in the 1970s and tended to be too optimistic throughout the last decades, with early forecasts predicting an important role for hydrogen as transport fuel by 2010 or even much earlier (Moriarty and Honnery, 2019). Hydrogen vehicles could significantly reduce GHG from transport, but the production of hydrogen is very costly and needs further research and development (Durbin and Malardier-Jugroot, 2013). There are still many unresolved questions regarding the production, distribution and storage of hydrogen (Gondal and Sahir, 2012). Passenger cars running on hydrogen are already commercially available in Germany and Austria, but hydrogen trucks are still in their prototype stage (Anderhofstadt and Spinler, 2019). Notably, it is predicted that hydrogen will predominantly be important for freight transport and not so much for passenger transport (Moriarty and Honnery, 2019). Already in the early 2000s it was recommended that the ecological benefits and cost efficiency would be higher if hydrogen was introduced for freight transport (Farrell *et al.*, 2003). The reason is that freight transport entails "a small number of relatively large vehicles that are operated by professional crews along a limited number of point-to-point routes or within a small geographic area" (Farrell *et al.*, 2003, p. 1357). Furthermore, heavy-duty vehicles are produced to order and each vehicle receives considerable engineering attention, which facilitates technological innovation (as compared to passengers cars which are manufactured in large quantities on assembly lines) (Farrell *et al.*, 2003).

Table 4.2 Impact and timeframe of alternative fuels for road freight transport. (based on Punte *et al.*, 2019)

GHG emissions reduction impact	Timeframe		
	Short (today–2022)	Medium (2023–2030)	Long (2031–2050)
High (>20%)	• Electric/hybrids urban		• Hydrogen and hydrogen-related fuels
Medium (10–20%)		• Electric/hybrids (long-haul)	
Low (<10%)	• Cleaner diesel • Biofuels • CNG • **LNG**		

The impact of LNG is estimated to be rather low and short-term according to Table 4.2. Apparently, conventional natural gas is still a fossil fuel and therefore not suitable to comply with the 2050 zero emission logistics targets of the European Union (Punte et al., 2019). Despite that, LNG can play an important role along the way to zero emission logistics in several respects. On the one hand, natural gas is considered to be a bridge fuel in the transition process from oil and coal to a (near-)zero emission energy system (Zhang et al., 2016). Though natural gas is fossil, it is the cleanest burning fossil fuel. The combustion of LNG causes nearly 99% less particulate matter (PM) and sulfur oxide (SO_x) emissions, around 80% less nitrogen oxides (NO_x) and around 20% less carbon dioxide compared to diesel (Kumar et al., 2011). Vehicles fueled with LNG also produce lower noise levels, which allows them to enter zones with driving bans, like specific inner cities or making deliveries at night time (Peters-von Rosenstiel et al., 2015). And most importantly, the LNG technology is already available and ready to use, as opposed to hydrogen. The first use of natural gas vehicles dates back to the 1930s, and today there is a wide range of natural gas vehicles available (Osorio-Tejada et al., 2015; Yeh, 2007). Using LNG trucks could be a first step to reduce emissions from freight transport until zero emission fuel cell trucks are mature and ready for the market. Recent literature also suggests that there are synergies between natural gas and hydrogen technology in a way that natural gas infrastructure could help enable a transition to the long-term application of hydrogen in transportation (Ogden et al., 2018). The synergies result from the fact that natural gas and hydrogen share some physical similarities (both can be stored as compressed gases or cryogenic liquids) and they use similar infrastructural components (such as compressors, storage tanks and pipelines) (Ogden et al., 2018). It is therefore being discussed whether natural gas infrastructure can be re-used or designed for compatibility with the emerging hydrogen technology to promote the introduction of hydrogen. For example, the existing natural gas pipeline network could be used to distribute hydrogen initially. Blending hydrogen and natural gas is technically possible up to a mix of 17% hydrogen (Gondal and Sahir, 2012). This way, the use of natural gas (and LNG) at present can promote the future deployment of zero emission fuels like hydrogen.

On the other hand, the environmental impact of LNG can be further improved if bio-methane from renewable sources is used to produce LNG. LNG made from bio-methane is then referred to as "renewable LNG" (r-LNG) or "bio-LNG". Fossil methane and bio-methane can be mixed to produce LNG. LNG purely made from bio-methane has the potential to reduce CO_2 emissions between 43–67%

(depending on the engine technology) as compared to diesel vehicles (Alamia *et al.*, 2016). Shell even announced that they are going to construct a liquefaction plant in Germany which enables them to provide CO_2-neutral bio-LNG in the upcoming years (Reichel, 2020). For the distribution of bio-methane the same infrastructure and networks as for LNG and CNG can be used. The risk associated with the introduction of bio-methane as alternative fuel is therefore expected to be limited (Thrän *et al.*, 2014). The production costs of renewable LNG are relatively high at the moment compared to the production costs of fossil LNG or diesel (Scheitrum *et al.*, 2017). However, it is estimated that bio-methane will become more widely available in the upcoming years due to advancements in biomass gasification technologies and integration with the distribution networks of LNG and CNG (Alamia *et al.*, 2016). Therefore, the use of LNG trucks could serve as a transitional solution until the large-scale production of bio-methane is possible at competitive price in the coming years (Osorio-Tejada *et al.*, 2017).

The above discussions show that LNG is currently the only viable alternative for heavy-duty vehicles and long-haul transportation. In some European countries, LNG is already a fully accepted technology. For example, the development stage of LNG as transport fuel in Spain, the Netherlands and the United Kingdom is estimated to be between demonstration and early market (Osorio-Tejada *et al.*, 2017). Nevertheless, in countries like Germany and Austria, the use of LNG is rather moderate and demand is fairly low except for some first pioneer users (Anderhofstadt and Spinler, 2019). It is therefore necessary to learn the reasons which cause the hesitation of the fleet owners and find measures to encourage the widespread adoption of LNG.

4.5   Comparison of the ASI Pillars

Sections 4.2–4.4 presented three different strategies for sustainable freight transport, each of which can be classified as a different pillar of the ASI approach. Table 4.3 gives an overview of the characteristics of these three strategies under further investigation in this thesis. As can be seen, a variety of specific strategies for sustainable freight transport are covered which allows the analysis and comparison of similarities as well as differences between the acceptance and promotion of these diverse strategies.

Table 4.3 Comparison of sustainable freight transport strategies in this thesis

ASI pillar	Implementation strategy	Underlying sustainability principle	Type of change	Transport distances
Avoid	Bundling enabled by horizontal collaboration in a PI network	*Sufficiency* > fewer transport ways = reduce transport	Organizational change	Short-long distance
Shift	Modal shift enabled by multimodality	*Consistency* > other transport ways = substitute road transport	Organizational & (partly) technological change	Mainly long distance
Improve	LNG as an alternative fuel	*Efficiency* > better transport ways = technological advancement	Technological change	Mainly medium-long distance

Environmental science adopts three basic principles that lead to sustainable development: sufficiency, consistency and efficiency. Each ASI pillar, and accordingly each implementation strategy under study in this thesis, is subject to one of the three principles. The avoid pillar is based on the *sufficiency principle*, which aims to lower the level of transports (Muller, 2008). "Sufficiency means more intensive utilization or shared utilization of goods" (Mauch *et al.*, 2001, p. 133). This is exactly what the PI network aims to achieve by means of horizontal collaboration: transport resources should be shared among all partners for a better overall utilization. Sufficiency is aimed at the change of human behavior. Human beings need to alter their lifestyles and move towards more sustainable patterns of consumption (Samadi *et al.*, 2017). The shift pillar is based on the *consistency principle*, where a certain level of transports should be provided using other, less polluting ways of transport. Consistency aims at fundamental changes in transport by substituting high emission transport modes like road transport with environmentally friendly modes (Samadi *et al.*, 2017). Multimodality is an example for realizing the consistency principle, as multimodality allows the shift of freight to more sustainable transport modes. The improve pillar is based on the *efficiency principle*, which rests on technological innovations to increase resource productivity and resource efficiency. According to the efficiency principle, a certain level of transport services should be provided with lower resource input (Muller, 2008). Notably, the introduction of improve/efficiency measures bears the risk of rebound effects. A rebound effect describes the paradox between resource efficiency and resource consumption (Wang and Lu, 2014). The efficiency gains of improved technologies may be offset due to changes of consumer behavior (for example, due to the introduction of alternative fuels for road vehicles the use of road transport may increase, which offsets the efficiency gains of alternative fuels) (Matos and Silva, 2011). There is widespread agreement that to achieve a sustainable development of the transport sector, a combination of all three principles (sufficiency, consistency and efficiency) will be needed (Muller, 2008; Mauch *et al.*, 2001). This thesis will therefore cover all three principles to compare them and gain knowledge about how to promote the implementation of the principles.

As regards the type of change, the strategies for sustainable freight transport either involve organizational change, technological change, or both. Horizontal collaboration in a PI network is subject to organizational change: Due to the collaboration, the transport organization is modified, e.g. transport requests are shared with others, transport capacities of collaborating partners can be taken into account etc., but there is no (substantial) additional technology required. Multimodality also involves organizational changes, as new transport modes and their requirements must be regarded in the transport organization (e.g. booking of train slots,…). Partly, multimodality may also involve technological change, for example infrastructure to enable smooth transition between transport modes (terminals, cranes, etc.). Alternative fuels such as LNG require technological change, as the transition towards alternative fuels is bound up with new technology like propulsion systems, fueling stations, etc.

Finally, the three strategies for sustainable freight transport under study in this thesis also cover a diverse range of transport distances. While bundling transport streams in a PI network is basically possible for every distance (short, medium and long distance), a modal shift is limited to long distance transport. A distance of 300 kilometers is suggested by the European Commission as the minimum where multimodal transport constitutes an economically feasible alternative (European Commission, 2011). Practitioners suggest that 500 kilometers is a more realistic minimum distance. The use of alternative fuels is possible for every type of distance (Table 4.1), but the use of LNG is particularly recommended for medium or long distances. This is due to the high energy density and the (currently) limited network of filling stations (Anderhofstadt and Spinler, 2019).

The Acceptance of Sustainable Freight Transport

5

5.1 Theoretical Background on Behavioral Intention and Technology Acceptance

In this subchapter, multiple theoretical perspectives are considered which are suitable to explain why logistics service providers are willing to implement sustainable freight transport strategies in theory. The conceptual framework illustrated in this subchapter provides the theoretical foundation for the second research question (Which determinants influence the acceptance of sustainable freight transport strategies?). The primary theory which informs the second research question is the technology acceptance Model (TAM) published by Davis (1989). TAM belongs to the group of so-called behavioral theories (Yuen *et al.*, 2017) which try to explain individuals' behavioral intention. In the following, the most prominent and widely used behavioral theories will be explained in detail.

5.1.1 Theory of Reasoned Action

Researchers aimed to estimate the acceptance of innovations and new technologies for decades. A very early and fundamental model which contributes to understanding the concept of acceptance is the "theory of reasoned action" (TRA), published by Fishbein and Ajzen (1975). TRA is considered to be one of the most influential models in the social and psychological literature (Staats, 2004). TRA aims to predict a person's intention to behave in a certain way. Fishbein and Ajzen postulate that behavioral intention will ultimately lead to behavior. According to TRA, there are two determinants which influence behavioral intention, namely the *attitude towards the behavior* on the one hand, and *subjective*

© The Author(s) 2022
S. Pfoser, *Decarbonizing Freight Transport*,
https://doi.org/10.1007/978-3-658-37103-6_5

norm on the other hand (Figure 5.1). The attitude represents an individual's tendency to assess the specific behavior as positive or negative (Ajzen and Fishbein, 1980). In the case of companies, attitude is often reflected in the companies' management philosophy (Yuen *et al.*, 2017). The management philosophy can promote or hamper sustainable business practices such as sustainable transport strategies. Subjective norm can be described as social influence or pressure which supports or impedes a particular behavior (Schepers and Wetzels, 2007). In the business context, subjective norms may be caused by shareholders or stakeholders who approve or disapprove specific business practices (Yuen *et al.*, 2017).

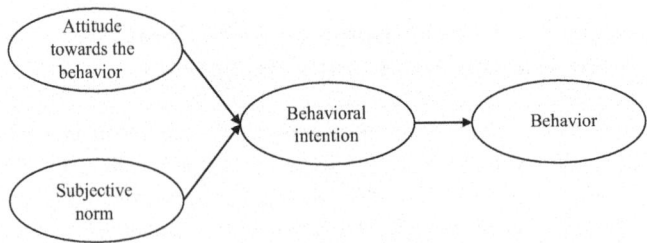

Figure 5.1   Theory of reasoned action. (Fishbein and Ajzen, 1975)

5.1.2   Theory of Planned Behavior

An important assumption of TRA is that individuals act upon volitional control, which means that they suppose to be able to perform the behavior whenever they are willing to do so (Madden *et al.*, 1992). However, behavioral control is often a variable determinant, as it is depending on the individual capabilities and opportunities of the person or company in charge (Staats, 2004). To address this aspect, Ajzen refined TRA and developed the theory of planned behavior (TPB; Ajzen, 1985; Ajzen, 1991). Compared to TRA, TPB additionally involves the construct *perceived behavioral control* (Figure 5.2). Perceived behavioral control describes the degree to which individuals believe they are able to accomplish a task or execute a behavior due to their

competences or external circumstances (Staats, 2004). Most often, sustainable strategies are also dependent on competences or external circumstances, e.g. knowledge or existing facilities. For example, LNG can only be used if there are refueling stations available, and realizing a modal shift requires knowledge about the organization of multimodal transport services. TPB therefore improves the understanding of why and how sustainable strategies are implemented.

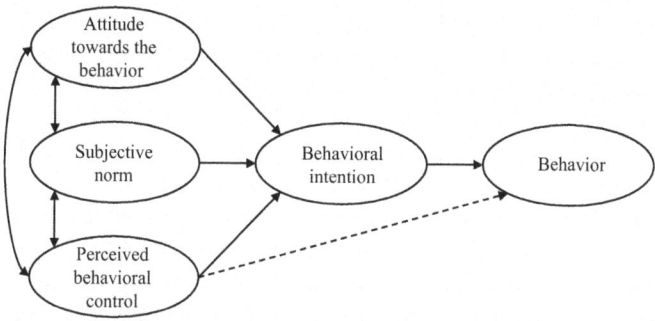

Figure 5.2 Theory of planned behavior. (Ajzen, 1991)

5.1.3 Technology Acceptance Model

One of the most influential and most widely used extensions of the theory of reasoned action (Fishbein and Ajzen, 1975) and the theory of planned behavior (Ajzen, 1991) is the technology acceptance model (Davis, 1989). According to Fishbein and Ajzens' work there is close coherence between attitude and behavior: Figure 5.1 and Figure 5.2 illustrate that behavioral intention, such as the intention to use a technology, is determined by a person's attitude. Davis (1989) specifies the construct "attitude toward using a technology" by introducing two external variables. These new variables are *perceived usefulness* and *perceived ease of use* (Figure 5.3). Perceived usefulness denotes the degree to which it is believed that using a particular system is advantageous to enhance the overall performance (Davis, 1989). Perceived ease of use is defined as "the degree to which a person believes that using a particular system would be free of effort" (Davis, 1989, p. 320). Davis claims that all else being equal, a technology is more likely to be accepted by users if its application is considered to be useful and easy to use.

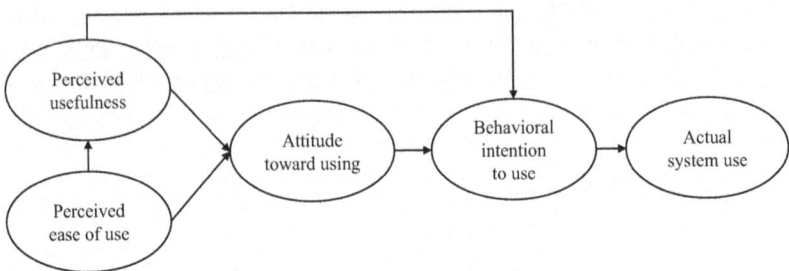

Figure 5.3 Technology acceptance model. (Davis, 1989)

Davis' technology acceptance model (TAM) originally focused on assessing the acceptance of information technology. By now TAM has already been employed on various other technologies from different research fields, as diverse as health care (Holden and Karsh, 2010), energy technologies (Chen *et al.*, 2017), pedagogy (Alharbi and Drew, 2014), nutritional science (Ronteltap *et al.*, 2008), and many more. A main advantage of TAM is that it is very simple and easy to use, yet a powerful model to explain users' technology acceptance (Lee *et al.*, 2003). TAM has been frequently applied in the context of transport and logistics. Manifold studies exist using TAM in context of sustainable transport strategies (Table 5.1). As can be seen in Table 5.1, TAM is suitable to explain the acceptance of avoid, shift as well as improve strategies for sustainable transport. Many studies refer to passenger transport, but TAM is also used to model the acceptance of innovations and technologies in freight transport. As a matter of fact, the majority of studies listed in Table 5.1 regard "improve strategies", which constitute technological innovations to achieve sustainability (see Chapter 4). For example, there are studies about alternative fuels acceptance (e.g. Hackbarth and Madlener, 2013; van Rijnsoever *et al.*, 2013) or truck platooning (Castritius *et al.*, 2020). The technology acceptance model is especially suitable to explain improve strategies, since TAM was originally designed to study technology acceptance. However, other studies also use TAM to assess the acceptance of avoid strategies (e.g. reducing transport by pooling rides or car-sharing; Wang *et al.*, 2018 and Geldmacher *et al.*, 2017) and shift strategies (e.g. modal shift towards public transport or bicycles; Chen and Chao, 2011 and Hazen *et al.*, 2015).

Table 5.1 List of studies using TAM in context of sustainable transport strategies

ASI pillar	Sustainable transport strategy	Reference	Determinants of acceptance (additional to the determinants proposed by Davis (1989))
avoid	Ride-sharing services	Wang et al. (2018)	Personal innovativeness, perceived risk, environmental awareness
	Car-sharing	Fleury et al. (2017)	Perceived environmental friendliness, effort expectancy, performance expectancy, facilitating conditions
		Geldmacher et al. (2017)	Social influence, effort expectancy, performance expectancy, facilitating conditions
shift	Public transport	Chen and Chao (2011)	Habit, perceived behavior control, subjective norm
	Public bicycle systems	Hazen et al. (2015)	Perceived convenience, perceived quality, perceived value
improve	Alternative fuel vehicles	Hackbarth and Madlener (2013)	Purchase price, fuel cost, CO_2 emissions, driving range, fuel availability, refueling time, battery recharging time, policy incentives
		van Rijnsoever et al. (2013)	Initial purchase price, fuel price, driving range, time to refuel, availability of fuel, local emissions
	Electric vehicles	Wang et al. (2016)	Environmental concern, attitude toward adopting a hybrid electric vehicle (HEV), subjective norm, perceived behavioral control, personal moral norm, intention to adopt a HEV

(continued)

Table 5.1 (continued)

ASI pillar	Sustainable transport strategy	Reference	Determinants of acceptance (additional to the determinants proposed by Davis (1989))
		Sang and Bekhet (2015)	Government intervention, environmental concern, performance attributes, social influence, financial benefits, demographic, infrastructure readiness
		Zhang et al. (2011)	Demographic variables, understanding of alternative fuel vehicles, experience, vehicle performance, government policy, environmental requirement, opinion of peers, vehicle price, tax reduction, fuel price, fuel availability, maintenance cost, vehicle safety
	Hydrogen vehicles	Huijts et al. (2014)	Intention to act, attitude towards acting, perceived effects of the technology, subjective norm, perceived behavioural control, personal norm, outcome efficacy, environmental problem perception, energy security problem perception, problem perception, trust in the municipality, trust in the industry, distributive fairness, positive affect, negative affect
		Tarigan et al. (2012)	Demographic variables, knowledge, environmental attitude, willingness to pay more to purchase hydrogen vehicles

(continued)

Table 5.1 (continued)

ASI pillar	Sustainable transport strategy	Reference	Determinants of acceptance (additional to the determinants proposed by Davis (1989))
		Kang and Park (2011)	Psychological needs, perception towards hydrogen fuel cell vehicles, values, experience
		Thesen and Langhelle (2008)	Demographic variables, hydrogen support, environmental and hydrogen knowledge, attitude
		Zachariah-Wolff and Hemmes, 2006	Demographic variables, knowledge, perception, attitude
		O'Garra et al. (2005)	Demographic variables, environmental attitude, environmental knowledge, environmental behavior knowledge about hydrogen and fuel cells, attitude toward science and technology
		Schulte et al. (2004)	Perception of product, values of person in question, wants of person in question, needs of person in question, past experience, social background
	Natural gas vehicles	Pfoser et al. (2018d)	Accessibility/availability of technology and refueling stations, attitude towards alternative fuels and interest in LNG, safety concerns
		Jayaraman et al. (2015)	Refueling station availability, payback period, petrol price, refueling time
	Truck platooning	Castritius et al. (2020)	Image, driving safety, technology affinity, trust in automated systems

5.2   Determinants of Sustainable Freight Transport Acceptance

In the following subchapter, the determinants of sustainable freight transport acceptance will be elaborated. The technology acceptance model postulates that acceptance is determined by two main factors, namely usefulness and ease of use, which lead to a specific attitude about a system or technology. The aim of the following subchapter is to gain further insights on how usefulness and ease of use are formed in the context of sustainable transport strategies.

5.2.1   Overview / Comparison of Determinants

In Plasch *et al.* (2021), Pfoser (in press), Pfoser *et al.* (2016a) and Pfoser *et al.* (2018d) the factors which motivate (or hinder) logistics companies to implement sustainable freight transport strategies were elaborated. Each paper refers to one of the three ASI pillars: Plasch *et al.* (2021) describe the motives to enter a PI network, Pfoser (in press) analyzes the barriers to use multimodal freight transport, and Pfoser *et al.* (2018d) as well as Pfoser *et al.* (2016a) raise the determinants of LNG acceptance. In the following, the findings from the three papers will be juxtaposed to see what are the overarching determinants that influence the acceptance of sustainable freight transport strategies in general. Table 5.2 gives a comparison of the higher-level determinants which occur in context of PI, multimodality as well as LNG. There are some determinants which specify the usefulness of sustainable freight transport strategies, while other determinants specify the ease of using sustainable freight transport strategies (Figure 5.4). The following subchapters will describe the determinants in detail.

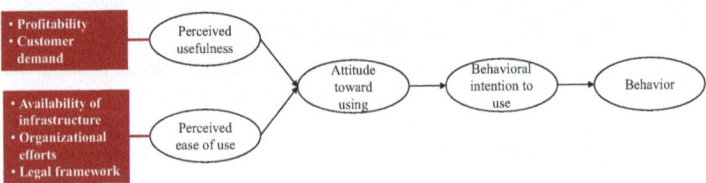

Figure 5.4 Technology acceptance model specified for sustainable freight transport strategies

Table 5.2 Determinants of sustainable freight transport acceptance

Determinant of sustainable freight transport acceptance	Avoid: Determinant in context of PI collaboration (cf. Plasch *et al.*, 2021)		Shift: Determinant in context of multimodality (cf. Pfoser, in press)		Improve: Determinant in context of LNG (cf. Pfoser *et al.*, 2016a and Pfoser *et al.*, 2018d)	
Profitability (~usefulness)	+ +	Cost reduction	+ +	Investment costs, shipment characteristics	+ +	Investment costs
Customer demand (~usefulness)			+ +	Request from customers	+ +	Request from customers
Availability of infrastructure (~ease of use)	+	No physical infrastructure but neutral IT platform	+ +	Multimodal terminals, railway sidings	+ +	Refueling stations
Organizational efforts (~ease of use)	+	Efficient orchestration and sharing mechanisms	+ +	Administrative effort, pre- and post-haulage	+	Route planning
Legal framework (~ease of use)	+ +	Data sharing policies, antitrust law	+ +	Licensing processes, railway regulations	+ +	Licensing processes

+ + ... *high relevance,* + ... *medium relevance*

5.2.2 Profitability

The determinant which is clearly the most important factor influencing the acceptance of sustainable freight transport strategies is profitability. Profitability influences the perceived usefulness of sustainable freight transport strategies. Hardly any LSPs would introduce sustainable transport practices without expecting a cost reduction, or at least cost neutrality as compared to their "business as usual" strategy. This finding holds for all three types of sustainable strategies under analysis in this thesis; avoid, shift and improve.

In the case of technological innovations such as LNG trucks, it is important for LSPs that the purchase cost of the assets amortize during the expected useful life (Pfoser *et al.*, 2016a). LSPs face significantly higher investment costs when building up an LNG fleet since LNG trucks cost around one third more than diesel trucks (Scania, 2020). To evaluate the profitability of their investment, LSPs usually consider the total cost of ownership (TCO) and not only the initial purchase price of an asset (Pfoser *et al.*, 2016a). The increased investment for LNG trucks can therefore be offset by low operational costs (e.g. lower fuel prices compared to diesel).

To implement multimodal freight transport there might also be some investments required, for example to acquire multimodal (craneable) loading units. The main focus of the profitability considerations in the context of multimodal transport is however not on investment costs but rather on shipment characteristics (Pfoser, in press). As a matter of fact, multimodality is not suitable for every type of shipment. Transport distances and cargo volumes influence the economic viability of multimodal operations. The efficiency of multimodal freight transport is rather limited on short distances, for low cargo volumes and for time-sensitive cargo (Guglielminetti *et al.*, 2017). LSPs and shippers therefore evaluate carefully before setting up multimodal routes. The importance of economic viability towards a modal shift is also reflected in a myriad of mode choice studies. Meixell and Norbis (2008), Flodén *et al.* (2017) and Pfoser *et al.* (2018c) conducted literature reviews to compare the results of mode choice studies and all of them found that cost is usually the most important determinant that occurs in every study on mode choice.

Entering horizontal collaboration in a PI network is usually not bound up with the purchase of new assets and investment costs, instead it is more of a strategic decision. However, also in this case profitability is the most important driving force that influences the decision to participate in a PI network (Plasch *et al.*, 2021). The commitment to horizontal collaboration is bound up with some sacrifices, for example sharing data, resources or customer orders with competing organizations (Pan *et al.*, 2019). In return for making these sacrifices, logistics companies expect to gain economic advantages such as cost savings or increased turnover. All case companies in Plasch *et al.* (2021) stressed that the reduction of logistics costs is of very high priority to them. Achieving these cost reductions by bundling capacities in a PI network is a strong incentive for them to collaborate.

It should be noted that environmental benefits are a "nice to have" but not a decisive determinant for LSPs to introduce sustainable practices (Pfoser *et al.*, 2016a). Most LSPs acknowledge that emission savings and other environmental benefits are well suited for marketing purposes ("green washing", McKinnon *et al.* (2015)), but what really matters for them is profitability. This came up very clearly in the context of all three sustainable freight transport strategies under study in this thesis. For example, during the in-depth interviews on multimodality, the respondent of LSP#4 affirmed:

"I am working for quite some time in the transport sector and the topic of green logistics has been discussed for about ten years now... but I can tell you that we never, ever, had a customer who was willing to pay one Euro more for the transport service just to reduce CO_2 emissions!"

This shows the limited importance that is put on environmental issues when deciding on a transport service, which is again confirmed by a vast number of mode choice studies (e.g. Flodén *et al.* (2017); Arencibia *et al.* (2015); Guilbault and Cruz (2010)). As stated by Flodén *et al.* (2017), the environmental impact in the selection process of a transport solution only accounts for 5% and is therefore only of minor importance for the acceptance of sustainable freight transport strategies.

5.2.3 Customer Demand

Implementing sustainable freight transport strategies can also be useful to meet the expectations and demand from customers and clients. For two types of sustainable transport strategy (multimodality and LNG) it turned out that requests from their customers constitute a main incentive for LSPs to introduce sustainable practices. In turn, if customers have a bad perception of sustainable freight transport strategies, LSPs will be reluctant to introduce these strategies (Pfoser, in press).

Pfoser *et al.* (2016a) found that an explicit customer request to use alternative fuels can be a main driver for LSPs to introduce LNG. Pfoser (in press) stated that customers' perception significantly influences the use of multimodal services. The reason is that it is the customer of the LSP (i.e. the shipper or cargo owner) who ultimately decides whether sustainable transport strategies are an option or not. If customers reject sustainable practices, then LSPs do not have an incentive to introduce these sustainable practices. This is also reflected in other studies which conclude that customer pressure strongly influence the green offerings of LSPs (e.g. Lin and Ho, 2011; Isaksson and Huge-Brodin, 2013; Chu *et al.*, 2019). Only for the PI it has not been found that a specific customer request supports the participation in a PI network. However, the general request for sustainable transport operations might encourage logistics companies to enter a PI network.

The empirical evidence collected within this thesis showed up where the case companies intended to implement sustainable transport strategies upon customer request. For example, a large manufacturer of commercial vehicles reported during the LNG focus group that a Dutch partner wanted them to construct an LNG refueling station at their company site in Austria. However, it turned out that the Dutch partner did not have enough transport volumes to fully utilize the refueling station. The internal plans to construct the refueling station were abandoned subsequently after the Dutch partner of the manufacturer withdrew their request. This example reveals that in the case of the manufacturer, the external request was the most decisive reason to implement LNG, and without this request the plans to implement LNG were abandoned. The same applies for multimodality. Out of ten LSPs which were asked about their intentions to use multimodal freight transport during the in-depth interviews, eight stated that this decision (at least partly) depends on their customers. For example, the respondent of LSP#10 stated:

"We completely adapt to the customer requirements. If the customer demands multimodal transport, we organize multimodal transport. In most cases, the customer defines a specific delivery date or specifies the price that he is willing to pay. Then we have to check whether multimodal transport meets these customer requirements."

5.2.4   Availability of Infrastructure

The availability of infrastructure is another determinant which influences the acceptance of all three sustainable freight transport strategies under evaluation in this thesis. A relevant difference between the three strategies is that for multimodality and LNG it is predominantly physical infrastructure that is needed, whereas for the PI no (additional) physical infrastructure is needed but rather a digital platform.

Infrastructure readiness plays an important role to promote market penetration and the acceptance of alternative fuels such as LNG. Refueling stations constitute the critical infrastructure which is necessary to introduce alternative fuels within LSPs' truck fleets (Pfoser *et al.*, 2018d). Arteconi and Polonara (2013) found that the use of LNG vehicles is directly related to the distance between the refueling infrastructure. At the moment, the density of the LNG refueling network is not very high, but it is continuously growing (Feldpausch-Jaegers *et al.*, 2016), which is beneficial for the acceptance of LNG.

In the case of multimodal freight transport, infrastructure such as multimodal terminals or railway sidings is required to operate multimodal services. This infrastructure often constitutes a crucial bottleneck hampering the uptake of multimodal transport due to low capacities and restricted opening hours (European Commission, 2011). Multimodal terminals are major nodes where all transport modes run together, thus they have an important role to facilitate a modal shift. If there is no infrastructure and equipment available to enable sufficient transshipment between the transport modes, the acceptance of multimodality is at risk (Pfoser, in press). Not only is physical infrastructure such as terminals crucial for the implementation of multimodal transport, but also digital infrastructure such as Information and communication technology (ICT) or intelligent transport systems (ITS). Various types of contextual information are required for an efficient organization of multimodal transports, e.g. data on weather, location of cargo, traffic information or potentially disturbances (Singh and van Sinderen, 2015). It is the task of ICT to provide high quality and standardized data that support multimodal transport decisions.

As mentioned above, the infrastructural requirements for establishing a PI network involve the set-up of a platform which acts as a neutral orchestrator. This neutral orchestrator can be described as a nonpartisan trustee, not involved in the operational activities, whose responsibility is to *"maximize the total synergy gains of the network while keeping its impartiality"* (Ciprés and de la Cruz, M. Teresa, 2019, p. 211). Essentially, without the neutral platform the performance of the PI network would be inferior and the acceptance of entering the PI network would be deterred.

Lacking the required infrastructure means that the ease of using sustainable freight transport is substantially reduced for LSPs. The provision of infrastructure for sustainable transport is often accompanied by a chicken-and-egg problem. This means that the supply of the relevant infrastructure (e.g. refueling stations, multimodal terminals or PI platform) is hampered by the fact that the demand for sustainable freight transport is quite low. At the same time, demand for sustainable freight transport is restrained because the relevant infrastructure is missing.

5.2.5 Organizational Efforts

Organizational efforts also influence how well a company accepts a sustainable freight transport strategy. If a sustainable practice is bound up with high organizational complexity, it decreases the ease of using this practice, and therefore acceptance will be limited.

Especially multimodal transport is bound up with increased organizational effort compared to the less sustainable option unimodal road transport (Pfoser, in press). The reason is that sustainable transport modes such as railways or inland waterways have a lower network density, which means that it is difficult to establish point-to-point connections using these modes. Therefore, pre-haulage and/or post-haulage have to be organized in the course of multimodal transport. Another organizational burden are administrative barriers, which occur especially in transnational multimodal transport (Pfoser *et al.*, 2018b). Customs procedures, inspection processes and other formalities are time consuming and inhibit the acceptance of multimodality (Pfoser, in press). LSP#7 (in-depth interview on multimodality) named some further organizational efforts that might occur:

„Compared to truck transport, multimodal transport is more complex because an increased number of players are involved and there are more interfaces to other organizations (e.g. railway companies) that you cannot influence.

Organizational efforts may also arise from horizontal collaboration in a PI network due to the transactions with partners (e.g. asset sharing, exchange of transport requests, etc.) (Plasch *et al.*, 2021). Although it is the task of the network orchestrator to minimize the organizational efforts for the partners collaborating, there may remain some organizational issues (for example setting up the initial collaboration agreement).

In connection to LNG there might be some organizational efforts resulting from the low network density of refueling stations and the driving range (which is still somewhat shorter than that of diesel trucks). Due to these circumstances, route planning might be more complex for LNG fueled trucks (Pfoser *et al.*, 2016a).

5.2.6 Legal Framework

The legal framework is another determinant which influences the acceptance of sustainable freight transport. Logistics companies expect clear regulatory guidelines which support the introduction of sustainable strategies and which create legal security. In general, harmonization among the EU member states is desirable to ensure consistent regulations for transnational transport operations. This applies, for example, to the approval procedures required to authorize LNG vehicles and infrastructure (Pfoser *et al.*, 2016a) or to the issuing of safety certificates for multimodal railway undertakings (Pfoser, in press). At the moment, the licensing processes are often long-winded and discourage the use of sustainable freight transport strategies. In the focus group on LNG it was stated by a liquid gas provider that the legal framework conditions constitute the main barrier for the uptake of LNG in Austria. Also in the focus group on multimodality it was discussed that legislation is a crucial determinant of multimodal transport acceptance. A complex legal framework basically impedes infrastructure investments, for example for refueling stations or multimodal terminals (Reis *et al.*, 2013).

Another legal issue that has a large impact on multimodal road-rail transport is the state regulation of railways. Unlike the US, where rail infrastructure is mostly privately owned, rail infrastructure in Europe is a publicly owned monopoly which hampers competition. This is problematic because competition is decisive in enhancing the performance of the railway system and ensuring efficiency in terms of costs, quality of service and investment plans (Smith *et al.*, 2018; Mortimer and Islam, 2014; Clausen and Voll, 2013). To address this problem, the European Commission already adopted four legislative railway packages which target the liberalization of the European railway market (Smith *et al.*, 2018). However, Austrian LSPs only noticed a few improvements towards the liberalization and are not very satisfied with the railway providers (Pfoser, in press).

In the case of a PI network, specific legal issues emerge from the horizontal collaboration between partners, for example from the obligation to share data within the PI network. Logistics companies may have distinct data policies, i.e. terms and conditions that restrict data sharing and open data. Cooperation agreements should be drafted among these logistics companies to contract peer-to-peer connections (Hofman *et al.*, 2016). Knol *et al.* (2014) describe different scenarios for data sharing among transport actors. They recommend restricted open access and non-obligatory data sharing patterns to encourage information exchange in global transport chains. Horizontal collaboration in the PI network may not only be hampered because stakeholders are reluctant to work together, but they may simply not even be allowed to work together due to antitrust policies and regulations (Geerlings *et al.*, 2017). Here, governments have to intervene and create legal security for shippers and LSPs to enable horizontal collaboration.

Policy Measures to Promote Sustainable Freight Transport

6

6.1 Theoretical Background on Organizational Management

Attempts at theory-building in sustainable SCM and logistics are to date rather scarce. Many papers in the field of sustainable SCM and logistics lack a theoretical lens to provide theoretical perspectives (Touboulic and Walker, 2015). Several authors stress the theoretical dearth in the field of sustainable SCM (Touboulic and Walker, 2015; Carter and Easton, 2011; Sarkis *et al.*, 2011). However, there are some popular organizational theories which were repeatedly used in the past to study problems related to sustainable SCM/logistics. In order to successfully employ policy measures which encourage organizations' environmental commitment, the fundamental principles of organizational management must be understood. The profound understanding of how a company works and knowledge on organizations' operational principles allow the setting of precise and target-oriented measures for sustainability. In this subchapter, multiple theoretical lenses are used to understand organizational management and derive implications on how to influence organizational behavior with suitable policy measures. The conceptual framework illustrated in this subchapter provides the theoretical foundation for the fourth research question (Which policy measures promote the implementation of sustainable freight transport strategies?).

Organizational theories aim to provide "a management insight that can help explain or describe organizational behaviors, designs, or structures" (Sarkis *et al.*, 2011, p. 2). A wide range of disciplines contributed to the development of organizational theories, among them sociology, psychology, economics, political science and engineering (Hatch, 2018). Several literature reviews exist which map the theoretical framework of sustainable SCM and logistics studies (e.g. Liu *et al.*,

© The Author(s) 2022
S. Pfoser, *Decarbonizing Freight Transport*,
https://doi.org/10.1007/978-3-658-37103-6_6

2018; Dubey *et al.*, 2017; Touboulic and Walker, 2015; Carter and Easton, 2011; Sarkis *et al.*, 2011; Carter and Rogers, 2008). The collection of theories presented in these literature reviews were examined carefully in the course of this thesis. Those theories which indicate how to motivate the implementation of sustainable practices (such as sustainable freight transport strategies) were chosen as relevant theoretical lenses. Table 6.1 describes the theories that were classified as relevant and gives examples of studies which borrow from these theories in the context of sustainable SCM/logistics/transport practices.

Eight theories were chosen as relevant for deriving indications on how to encourage sustainable practices. These eight theories can be classified according to three different dimensions related to organizational existence, namely (1) organizational obligations (2) organizational capabilities (3) organizational functioning. Figure 6.2 depicts the three dimensions and their related theories using a Venn diagram. A Venn diagram is a popular way to illustrate the three pillars of sustainability (economic, social and environmental performance) using three circles that intersect (Lozano, 2008). The overlap of all three circles in the center of the diagram represents truly sustainable performance (Figure 6.1). An overlap of two circles represents partial sustainability and is referred to as equitable, bearable or viable performance (Figure 6.1). The three organizational dimensions (obligations, capabilities and functioning) each represent one of the three pillars of sustainability (economic, social and environmental) and thus can be also depicted using a Venn diagram.

Figure 6.1 Venn diagram illustrating the three pillars of sustainability. (based on Dalal-Clayton and Bass, 2002)

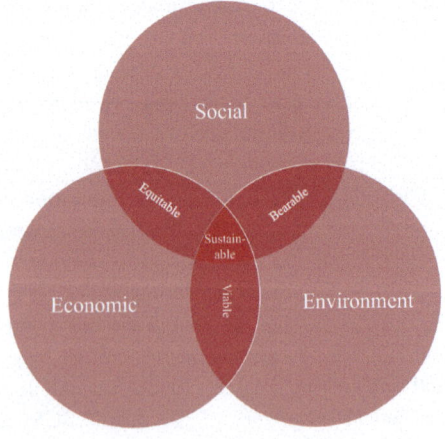

Organizational obligations represent *social* responsibility which organizations have towards their stakeholders. Organizational functioning constitutes the operational principles of organizations' performance which are predominantly based on *economic* considerations. And finally, organizational capabilities refer to the capacities and resources that organizations have access to, which are often limited by *environmental* conditions. Since the three dimensions of organizational obligations, capabilities and functioning each represent one of the sustainability pillars, they can also be classified according to equitable, bearable, viable and sustainable practices. For example, practices that comply with organizational obligations and organizational functioning are referred to as equitable in Figure 6.2. Practices that comply with organizational obligations and organizational capabilities are referred to as bearable, and practices that comply with organizational functioning and organizational capabilities are referred to as viable. In the following, each organizational dimension and their associated theories will be explained in detail. Later, in Subchapter 6.3.5, the theories will be used to support the policy measures for sustainable freight transport.

Figure 6.2 Theoretical framework to explain the adoption of sustainable freight transport strategies

6.1.1   Organizational Obligations

Several theories exist which refer to the companies' relationship to other organizations and the resulting obligations. Within their corporate activities, companies have to satisfy the needs of several parties, not only shareholders (owners), but also other stakeholders like governments, industrial interest groups, NGOs, customers, and society as a whole (Sen and Cowley, 2013). The *stakeholder theory* (Freeman, 1984) illustrates the responsibility of organizations to meet the expectations of their manifold stakeholders. These expectations also involve environmental concerns of stakeholders. Stakeholder theory is one of the most used theories in the context of sustainable SCM (Touboulic and Walker, 2015). Stakeholder theory postulates that stakeholder pressure influences the sustainable behavior of organizations. If stakeholders express environmental needs, then organizations tend to introduce sustainable strategies (Yuen *et al.*, 2017). The *agency theory* (Eisenhardt, 1989) uses a similar approach to explain companies' environmental engagement. The essence of agency theory is that one organization (the principal) authorizes another organization (the agent) to act on behalf of the principal (Sarkis *et al.*, 2011). Within their role as agents, companies are obligated to meet the sustainability concerns of the principals (Berrone and Gomez-Mejia, 2009). Principals may use incentives (such as reward systems) to stimulate pro-environmental behavior (Cordeiro and Sarkis, 2008).

Additionally the *institutional theory* (DiMaggio and Powell, 1983) is helpful to understand how companies can be motivated towards more sustainable behavior. According to the institutional theory, coercive, normative and mimetic pressures constitute an incentive that drives sustainable transport practices or discourage unsustainable transport practices (Morali and Searcy, 2013). Environmental regulations represent an example of coercive pressure. Coercive pressure often comes from governments or government agencies (Rivera, 2004). In contrast, normative pressure is mostly caused by customer and market requirements (Zhu *et al.*, 2013). Mimetic pressure appears when an organization imitates the actions of successful competitors (e.g. "green champions") in the same industry (Sancha *et al.*, 2015).

6.1.2   Organizational Capabilities

Several theories related to resources describe companies' capabilities to adopt sustainable strategies. The *resource-based view* (RBV) claims that companies gain a competitive advantage through their valuable, rare, inimitable and non-substitutable resources (Barney, 1991; Wernerfelt, 1984). In terms of sustainable transport practices, RBV teaches us that specific resources are required to enhance the environmental, social and economic performance in the supply chain (Touboulic and Walker, 2015). Aiming for sustainable business activities and greening the supply chain is also an opportunity to gain a competitive advantage (for example via differentiation and increased market power) (Sarkis *et al.*, 2011). In this context, knowledge resources and organizational learning provide additional important capabilities which enable sustainable transport practices (*knowledge-based view*, Grant, 1996). Green knowledge, sometimes also called green intellectual capital, is a fundamental resource which provides the basis for dynamic capabilities needed in unstable, competitive business environments (Wu, 2010). The *natural-resource-based view* (NRBV, Hart, 1995) is an extension of RBV which accounts for the fact that the natural environment may constitute a severe constraint for creating a competitive advantage. As early as 1995, the originator of NRBV anticipated that "it is likely that strategy and competitive advantage in the coming years will be rooted in capabilities that facilitate environmentally sustainable economic activity—a natural-resource-based view of the firm" (Hart, 1995, p. 991). Today, with the ever-increasing rise of the climate change, this statement holds true even more (Hart and Dowell, 2011).

The theories on organizational capabilities described above demonstrate that different types of resources enable (or limit) the organizational potential for sustainable action. Thus, it can be expected that supporting companies to gain the required resources for sustainable practices will motivate them towards environmental engagement (Morali and Searcy, 2013).

6.1.3 Organizational Functioning

Transaction cost economics and resource dependence theory are two theories which explain organizational functioning, i.e. the principles outlining how companies work or operate in a proper way. The basic assumption of *transaction cost economics* (TCE) is that two organizations engaged in a business activity incur costs as well as efforts (Williamson, 1981). Their goal is to establish management instruments and control systems such as contractual arrangements to minimize their transaction costs (Touboulic and Walker, 2015). Several elements of TCE can be utilized to explain decisions on investments and strategies towards sustainable transport practices (Sarkis *et al.*, 2011). The most evident implication of TCE is that the occurrence of transaction costs has an impact on the acceptance of sustainable practices (Touboulic and Walker, 2015). According to TCE, organizations are going to evaluate carefully the actual costs on different types

Table 6.1 Theories explaining the occurrence of sustainable freight transport practices

Theory and originator	Originating discipline	Organizational dimension	Implications for the promotion of sustainable freight transport	Studies using the theory in context of sustainable SCM/transport
Agency theory (Eisenhardt, 1989)	Economics, sociology, political science	Organizational obligations	Within their role as agents, companies can be motivated by principals to show environmental engagement (e.g. through reward systems)	Lozano et al. (2015); van Hoof and Lyon (2013); Berrone and Gomez-Mejia (2009); Cordeiro and Sarkis (2008)
Institutional theory (DiMaggio and Powell, 1983; Scott, 1987; Oliver, 1991)	Sociology, psychology	Organizational obligations	Institutional structures (e.g. rules, norms or routines) elicit external pressure for a company to act sustainably	Yang (2018); Dubey and Bag (2013); Morali and Searcy (2013); Zhu et al. (2013)
Knowledge-based view (Grant, 1996)	Strategic management	Organizational capabilities	The green intellectual capital or green knowledge of a company enables environmental protection	Schrettle et al. (2014); Aguilera-Caracuel et al. (2012); Sheu and Chen (2012)
(Natural-) resource based view (Wernerfelt, 1984; Barney, 1991; Hart, 1995)	Strategic management, micro-economics	Organizational capabilities	Key resources are required to achieve a sustainable performance in the supply chain. Pro-environmental practices could lead to a competitive advantage	Lozano et al. (2015); Morali and Searcy (2013); Guang Shi et al. (2012); Gold et al. (2010)

(continued)

Table 6.1 (continued)

Theory and originator	Originating discipline	Organizational dimension	Implications for the promotion of sustainable freight transport	Studies using the theory in context of sustainable SCM/transport
Resource dependence theory (Pfeffer and Salancik, 1978; Ulrich and Barney, 1984)	Sociology, political science	Organizational functioning	Organizations need to cooperate with others because they depend on resources from outside parties to realize sustainable practices	Yuen et al. (2017); Caniëls et al. (2013); Morali and Searcy (2013); Shang et al. (2010)
Stakeholder theory (Freeman, 1984; Donaldson and Preston, 1995)	Business ethics	Organizational obligations	Stakeholder pressure influences sustainable behavior > sustainable strategies are taken to meet stakeholders' environmental needs	Yuen et al. (2017); Lozano et al. (2015); Morali and Searcy (2013); Sen and Cowley (2013); Kim and Lee (2012);
Transaction cost economics (Williamson, 1981)	Economics	Organizational functioning	The occurrence of transaction costs has an impact on the acceptance of sustainable practices	Meinlschmidt et al. (2018); Barari et al. (2012); Chaabane et al. (2012); King (2007)

of transactions of decisions and practices within sustainable business activities (Sarkis *et al.*, 2011). Sustainable standards are more likely to be implemented if they improve the transaction costs in the supply chain (Rosen *et al.*, 2002).

Resource dependence theory (RDT, Pfeffer and Salancik, 1978) postulates that organizations are dependent on external parties' resources to increase their performance and sustain long-term benefits. Organizations will therefore seek collaboration with other partners to attain the resources they are dependent on (Ulrich and Barney, 1984). Applying RDT to the adoption of sustainable transport practices implies that organizations must carefully manage their dependence on external resources such as enabling technologies, distribution channels, standards or procedures (Sarkis *et al.*, 2011). The quality and effectiveness of collaboration with other partners will influence the success of implementing sustainable strategies (Shang *et al.*, 2010). Another aspect of resource dependence is that collaborating partners develop increased power over smaller organizations, and they tend to develop environmentally sound practices which will later also be adopted by the smaller organizations (González *et al.*, 2008). It can be concluded that enabling the effective collaboration and resource exchange between partners would be an efficient measure to encourage sustainable practices (Morali and Searcy, 2013).

6.2 Market Failures in Sustainable Freight Transport

The empirical investigation (interviews, focus group discussions) in the course of this thesis revealed that many problems related to sustainable freight transport are a result of market failures. Market failures are caused by the fact that individuals usually follow their self-interest and make the correct decision for themselves, instead of taking into account what is best for the whole group of individuals (Ledyard, 2008). In many cases, the individuals' decisions are not optimal from the societal point of view, which leads to market failures (Krugman and Wells, 2017). The Industry Commission (1998) underlined that the existence of market failures can be combated by policies that achieve better outcomes for society as a whole. Therefore, in this subchapter the main market failures which influence sustainable freight transport practices will be presented to show which problems have to be addressed by policy measures.

6.2.1 Tragedy of the Commons

The transportation system involves both, individual goods (e.g. transport assets such as trucks) and common goods (e.g. the environment or atmosphere)

(Richardson, 2005). The problem is that if private organizations such as logistics companies make any investments towards sustainable innovations, the value of this investment will most probably benefit third parties, such as society more than the organization itself (Richardson, 2005). For example, if an LSP purchases a truck which emits fewer emissions, the LSP has to bear the expenses for this investment although it only obtains a small share of the benefit (i.e. better air quality). Therefore, there is little motivation for organizations to realize sustainable transport policies because there is a disparity between the costs incurred and the benefits gained (Howes *et al.*, 2017).

The problem described is an example of the tragedy of the commons (Hardin, 1968). The tragedy of the commons predicts that common resources will suffer from overconsumption, under-investment and ultimately the depletion of the common resource due to the fact that others cannot be excluded from using the resource (Burger and Gochfeld, 1998; Faysse, 2005). Common resources are not owned by any individuals but by society as a whole, and this causes individuals to exploit the common resources to a degree that is inefficient at the collective level (Faysse, 2005). Although it would be desirable from the collective viewpoint to protect the common resources from overconsumption, it is economically irrational for an individual player (e.g. a company) to do so (Engel and Saleska, 2005). Market mechanisms have to appropriately manage the common resources to ensure that they are not reaped beyond their carrying capacity (Jenkins, 2002). Since the markets currently fail to do so, government regulations are necessary to address this problem. One participant of the multimodality focus group put it in a nutshell:

"Governmental regulation is absolutely needed to manage the consumption of natural resources and handle the problem of air pollution. If there were no regulations which restrict the maximum permitted speed, everyone would speed on the roads. The same applies to environmental issues—no company would consider them unless they are forced to."

Regulating the consumption of the commons is something that has to be implemented on a transnational level, otherwise no efficient results will be obtained.

6.2.2 Existence of Externalities

The transport sector is responsible for a multitude of negative externalities which are currently not sufficiently reflected in transport prices. These negative externalities include emissions, congestion, accidents, noise, vibration and other harmful effects which negatively affect third parties (Demir *et al.*, 2015). Prices aim to deliver a market equilibrium, but due to the existence of externalities in the transport market, the prices will lead to an inefficient resource allocation (Figure 6.3). In theory, negative externalities lead to market volumes that are too high because the prices are too low (Pindyck and Rubinfeld, 2013). In the transport sector, the excess volumes caused by the negative externalities are perfectly illustrated in practice by road congestion.

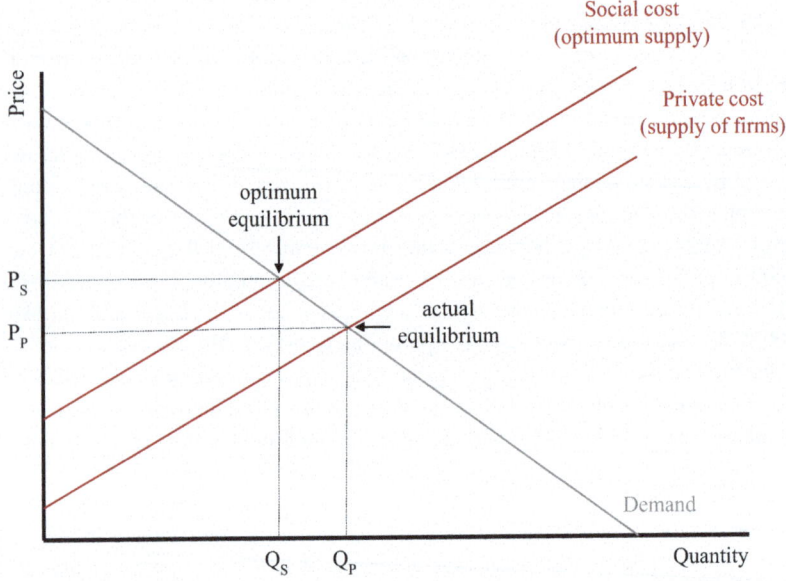

Figure 6.3 Microeconomic effects of negative externalities. (based on Pindyck and Rubinfeld, 2013)

Internalizing negative externalities is therefore an important task for policy to take on. This was also discussed during the focus group on multimodality. One participant of the multimodality focus group stated very clearly:

"The internalization of external costs is much more appropriate to create an economic incentive than the introduction of subsidies for multimodal transport. The reason is that subsidies rather distort competition while the internalization of external costs reflect the true cost of transport"

The other participants of the focus group strongly shared this opinion and recommended that politicians should make intensive efforts to internalize the external costs of road transport. The participants of the focus group stated that subsidies would cause controversy and dissent about the foundation for granting the subsidies. For example, the truck lobby associations will complain if railways receive funding from politics. However, if the "polluter pays" principle comes into effect, there is a clear rationale for the reallocation of economic burden. This will create a level playing field between all transport modes and make external costs part of the decision-making process of shippers (van Essen *et al.*, 2019).

6.2.3 Information Failure

Information failure is another type of market failure that occurs in many different markets, including the transport and logistics market. There exist two main types of information failure: asymmetric information and imperfect information (Pindyck and Rubinfeld, 2013). Asymmetric (or unbalanced) information occurs if one party has more knowledge than the other party within a business transaction. This may lead to opportunistic behavior of the party with advanced knowledge (Sinnandavar *et al.*, 2018). In context of sustainable freight transport, imperfect information is more relevant than asymmetric information. Imperfect information refers to the situation where a party does not have all the information required to make an informed business decision (Pindyck and Rubinfeld, 2013). Due to imperfect information, in many cases it is difficult for the logistics companies to understand the importance of sustainable transport (Chen *et al.*, 2018). A lack of efficient information and knowledge leads to incomplete markets where the resources are allocated insufficiently (Pratt and Phillips, 2000). The information failure is caused by the fact that it is hard for logistics companies to capture relevant information on sustainable freight transport solutions. Due to the lack of knowledge and information, an investment into sustainable strategies is perceived as risky by logistics companies, which leads to under-investment for sustainability (Nakamura *et al.*, 2003).

The problem of insufficient information was discussed during the focus group on multimodality. A shipper from the plastics industry stated that it is tremendously difficult for him to find information about multimodal transport offers. The participants agreed that multimodal transport is more complex than unimodal truck transport, and many companies are therefore reluctant to implement multimodality since they lack the required information. There also seems to be some kind of information asymmetry between the shippers (i.e. the cargo owners) and the freight forwarding companies. The shipper from the plastics industry reported that he tried to get transport offers from several multimodal transport operators, but these refused to inform him since they only deal with requests from freight forwarding companies. Due to these information failures, the implementation of sustainable transport strategies is inhibited in the logistics industry.

6.2.4   Free-rider Behavior

A free-rider problem occurs when costs and benefits of a strategy or action are not distributed equally among the parties involved (Pindyck and Rubinfeld, 2013). Implementing sustainable freight transport strategies is a typical scenario which creates an opportunity for free-riding. If one organization takes measures to reduce the ecological impact of transport, it incurs the costs of this measure but it will not fully obtain the benefits since other organizations gain the benefit as well, whether or not they set own sustainability measures (Engel and Saleska, 2005). The free-rider problem is similar to the tragedy of the commons, but it can also occur with goods that are non-rival and non-excludable in use, for example knowledge (Pindyck and Rubinfeld, 2013).

Horizontal collaboration between partners often involves the risk of free-rider behavior, for example because one partner may invest into assets (e.g. ICT systems), and the other partner may benefit from these investments without adequately sharing the costs (van der Horst and Langen, 2008). Efficient gain-sharing mechanisms must therefore be set up to allocate the benefits and prevent partners from free-riding. LSP#1 from the PI case study explains his expectations about a gain-sharing mechanism:

"Fair accounting should be achieved—executed by a neutral entity—with agreed unit prices, as well as with transparent and flexible pricing models"

6.3   Policy Measures to Promote Sustainable Freight Transport

The following subchapter presents policy measures that are (from the logistics companies' point of view) suitable to promote sustainable transport. These policy measures were developed within the focus groups of different projects on the topics of PI, multimodality and LNG. Several measures proved to be relevant for all three pillars of sustainable freight transport (avoid, shift, improve). These overarching measures will be presented below.

6.3.1   Overview / Comparison

In Plasch *et al.* (2021), Pfoser (in press), Pfoser *et al.* (2016a) and Pfoser *et al.* (2018d) it was elaborated which policy measures and/or success factors encourage logistics companies to implement sustainable freight transport strategies. Each paper refers to one of the three ASI pillars: Plasch *et al.* (2021) describe the success factors of a PI network, Pfoser (in press) analyzes policy measures to promote multimodal freight transport, and Pfoser *et al.* (2018d) as well as Pfoser *et al.* (2016a) raise policy measures and enablers to facilitate LNG as an alternative truck fuel. Together, these publications allow for a comparison of the policy measures that promote sustainable transport. The comparison of policy measures of different ASI pillars is illustrated in Table 6.2.

As described above, environmental policy theories refer to three types of policy measures- sticks, carrots and sermons (see 2.2 Typology of policy measures). An important implication resulting from the user-centric approach in this study is that logistics companies do not favor command & control measures (i.e. sticks) to promote sustainable freight transport. As can be seen in Table 6.2 no regulations or other command & control measures were proposed in any of the focus groups. Instead, another type of measures arose which is not covered by the common threefold sticks-carrots-sermons typology. This new type of measures involves the provision of basic infrastructure and framework conditions needed to use sustainable freight transport. The provision of infrastructure and other framework conditions is referred to as "means" in Table 6.2. At first glance, the instrument *means* shares some similarities with regulations and economic incentives. This is because, on the one hand, means can be provided by enacting laws and regulations (e.g. to create favorable legal conditions for sustainable transport) and on the other hand, means can be provided by using monetary resources (e.g. for infrastructure development). Despite these similarities, there are attributes that clearly distinguish means from sticks and carrots. The regulations that are issued to provide means do not force logistics companies to implement sustainable freight transport. They still have the freedom to choose whether they want to implement sustainable transport strategies. Thereby, means are different from sticks. And second, as opposed to economic incentives, the monetary resources that are spent on means are not intended to make it cheaper or more expensive for logistics companies to implement sustainable freight transport. Instead, the monetary resources are intended to *enable* logistics companies to implement sustainable freight transport. Therefore, means are also different from economic incentives.

Table 6.2 Policy measures to promote sustainable freight transport

Policy measure	Type	Avoid: Measure suitable to promote PI collaboration (cf. Plasch et al., 2021)	Shift: Measure suitable to promote multimodality (cf. Pfoser, in press)	Improve: Measure suitable to promote LNG (cf. Pfoser et al., 2016a and Pfoser et al., 2018d)
Monetary instruments	Carrots		+ + Internalization of external costs	+ + Security of investment, subsidies, R&D funds
Infrastructure development	Means	+ Open used infrastructure	+ + Increased capacity of multimodal terminals, better railway interoperability	+ + Refueling station network
Information & transparency	Means	+ + Enforce full network transparency	+ + Track performance, establish a one-stop-shop for multimodal bookings	
Adaptation of legal framework	Means	+ + Antitrust laws	+ + Harmonization of rail standards, increased weight limits	+ + Simplification of concession processes
Awareness raising	Sermons	+ + Trust-building measures	+ + Information campaigns, roadshows	+ + Demonstration of technology
Education & training	Sermons		+ + Courses, training sessions	+ + Mobilization of pioneer users

+ + ... *high relevance*, + ... *medium relevance*

To conclude, the new typology suggested to effectively promote sustainable freight transport strategies would be carrots-means-sermons instead of sticks-carrots-sermons (Figure 6.4). In this new typology, carrots can be considered the most restrictive and sermons the least restrictive measure. In the following subsections, the three types of measures suggested to promote sustainable freight transport will be presented in detail.

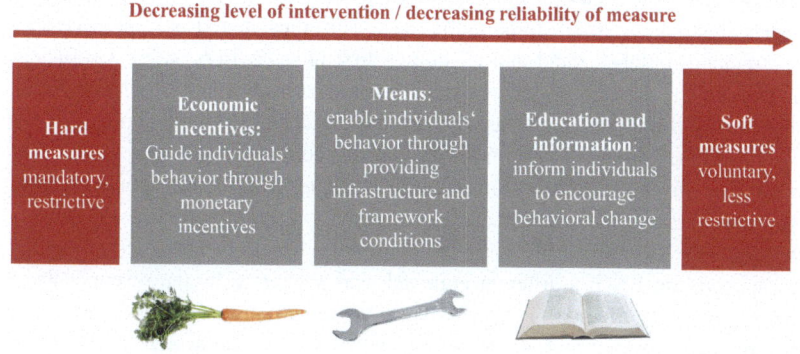

Decreasing level of intervention / decreasing reliability of measure

| Hard measures mandatory, restrictive | Economic incentives: Guide individuals' behavior through monetary incentives | Means: enable individuals' behavior through providing infrastructure and framework conditions | Education and information: inform individuals to encourage behavioral change | Soft measures voluntary, less restrictive |

Figure 6.4 Classification of user-centric policy measures for sustainable freight transport

6.3.2   Carrots for Sustainable Freight Transport

The implementation of sustainable transport strategies can be quite capital-intensive. The first (and from logistics companies' point of view most important) category of policy measures for sustainable freight transport is therefore carrots, i.e. monetary incentives. Monetary incentives address the fundamental need of logistics companies for profitability (see explanations in 5.2.2).

In the context of LNG, subsidies and grants constitute important monetary instruments to foster logistics companies' investment into LNG fueled vehicles (Pfoser *et al.*, 2018d). The higher investment cost of LNG fueled trucks is one of the main barriers for fleet operators because the acquisition of alternatively fueled vehicles has to pay off for them (Pfoser *et al.*, 2016a; Ma *et al.*, 2013). Receiving funding for LNG vehicles from the public sector is therefore a fundamental driving force that encourages logistics companies to start up LNG fleets (Engerer and Horn, 2010; Osorio-Tejada *et al.*, 2015; Wang *et al.*, 2015). Governments have different options to incentivize LNG usage with monetary instruments. On the one hand, they can support the fuel price by granting tax advantages for LNG, which makes LNG cheaper as compared to diesel (Yeh, 2007). This is already practiced in several European countries (Peters-von Rosenstiel et al., 2015). On the other hand, the purchase price of LNG vehicles could be subsidized by investment bonuses or loans. This has also been realized in some European countries, for example in Sweden an investment subsidy of €17,000 per truck was granted (Peters-von Rosenstiel et al., 2015) and in Germany an investment subsidy of €12,000 per truck was recently announced and already used by several companies (Landwehr, 2020). Importantly, these subsidies should only be necessary to stimulate initial demand and encourage first pioneer users. After a sufficient increase of the demand has taken place, the production volumes of LNG vehicles should rise to such an extent that the purchase prices fall (Pfoser et al., 2018d).

Also in the context of multimodality logistics companies emphasized that economic incentives are of utmost importance for them. Out of ten respondents from the interviews, eight affirmed that cost reduction is a very important or an important measure to increase the share of multimodal transport. However, compared to the study on LNG, a different approach was suggested by the respondents to reduce the costs of multimodal transport. In the focus group it was discussed that neither subsidies nor grants should be offered as monetary incentives to promote multimodal transport, but instead the external costs of transport should be internalized appropriately (Pfoser, in press). The reason is that subsidies distort competition while the internalization of external costs reflects the true cost of transport according to the "polluter pays" principle. An internalization of external costs would be in favor of the sustainable transport modes, including multimodal transport. Since the main variable of mode choice is transport price (Pfoser et al., 2018c), it would be highly efficient if transport prices are based on true-cost pricing and thus fully reflect external costs (Mostert and Limbourg, 2016). The internalization of external costs aims to create a level playing field between all transport modes such that external costs become part of the decision-making process in the logistics industry. At the moment, road transport is too cheap because it does not reflect the emissions, noise, congestion etc. that it causes (van Essen et al., 2019). This is why road transport dominates in the transport sector. In the focus group on multimodal transport, the internalization of external costs was rated as the most feasible and at the same time also the most effective policy measure to promote a modal shift, it is therefore considered as a high-impact measure (Pfoser, in press).

The remaining ASI pillar, avoid, does not require any economic policy measures. This is related to the fact that no additional assets or infrastructure are needed for the avoid strategies such as horizontal collaboration. Though profitability is equally important for horizontal logistics collaboration as well, it is expected that cost savings will result from bundling of transport streams and economies of scale (Plasch *et al.*, 2021; Vanovermeire *et al.*, 2014). Additional external monetary incentives are not necessary from the logistics companies' point of view.

6.3.3 Means for Sustainable Freight Transport

The empirical investigation revealed that logistics companies desire three different means that support the implementation of sustainable freight transport: Infrastructural development, information & transparency and adaptation of the legal framework.

Infrastructural development is relevant for all three ASI pillars, especially for multimodality and LNG. Multimodal transport requires sufficient terminals that combine different modes of transport (Šakalys and Batarliené, 2017; Kreutzberger and Konings, 2016). LNG requires an appropriate network of refueling stations (Osorio-Tejada *et al.*, 2017; Chang *et al.*, 2008). According to the logistics companies, governmental authorities should support the development of this infrastructure by putting forward development plans and funding the construction (Pfoser *et al.*, 2018d; Pfoser, in press). Importantly, logistics companies claim not only new and additional infrastructure needs to be built, but also the existing infrastructure should be improved by efficiency gains. As a matter of fact, the number of multimodal terminals is considered to be appropriate at the moment, but proper planning, extended opening hours and increased utilization are measures advised to improve existing infrastructure (Pfoser, in press). Also horizontal collaboration in the PI requires infrastructure, but as mentioned before, this infrastructure will not be newly constructed, but instead used in a different way. Specifically, warehouses and transport capacities will be used in an open and shared way by logistics companies (Vanovermeire *et al.*, 2014). Policy measures can present an impetus for companies to start thinking about sharing warehouses and other logistics infrastructure, although policy measures alone may not be sufficient to convince logistics companies to open their infrastructure to others. This is because the strategic alliance with (potential) competitors is a radical change for companies. The preferential treatment of horizontal logistics collaborations in tender procedures may constitute a measure to encourage the PI.

Promoting information and transparency is another measure that is suitable to support sustainable freight transport, namely the two pillars avoid and shift.

For horizontal collaboration to work, full network transparency is a vital feature for logistics companies. Political authorities can advance the occurrence of full network transparency by enforcing the monitoring of the PI performance. This monitoring can be accomplished by establishing control levers for tracing and documenting operational process performance in the PI network, e.g. delivery time and quality (Plasch et al., 2021). In the case of multimodality, tracking transport performance to allow for quality improvements and increased reliability of the service is also an important issue raised by the logistics companies (Pfoser, in press). In the focus group on multimodality, participants affirmed that they would highly appreciate the establishment of a one-stop-shop to make multimodal operations more flexible and easy-to-use (Pfoser, in press). The focus group participants rated this measure to be the second most important for promoting a modal shift. Various types of information can be transmitted in such a one-stop-shop, e.g. customs related data, estimated time of arrival or frequency of service (Islam et al., 2016). Another function is to comprehensively inform new entrants about the multimodal offers and make the booking of multimodal services as easy as booking road transport.

The adaption of the legal framework is a means that is expected to facilitate all three pillars of sustainable freight transport. Horizontal collaboration in a PI network needs an appropriate legal framework, since logistics companies may not be allowed to work together due to antitrust policies and regulations (Geerlings et al., 2017). Here, governments have to intervene and create legal certainty to enable horizontal collaboration (Pfoser et al., in press). For multimodal transport, a harmonization of the rail standards would be highly beneficial due to the fact that currently the multimodal business suffers from a variety of different standards among the European countries (Pfoser, in press). Another legal adaptation suggested to promote multimodality is increased weight permissions (e.g. increased maximum permissible weight for multimodal pre- and post-haulage or increased axle loads for railways). An increased permissible total weight reduces the number of transshipments and hence the cost per metric ton (Mortimer and Islam, 2014; Rodrigue and Notteboom, 2010). To promote LNG, a simplification of the concession processes is suggested as a useful measure (Pfoser et al., 2016a). Since LNG is classified as a dangerous good, the admission procedures are cumbersome and bureaucratic (Osorio-Tejada et al., 2017). Authorities can harmonize and simplify the application formalities and thus support the dissemination of LNG technology. Furthermore, the legal framework regarding safe storage, handling and bunkering of LNG needs to be harmonized since there are currently gaps and differences among various countries across the world (Aneziris et al., 2020).

6.3.4 Sermons for Sustainable Freight Transport

The third category of measures to promote sustainable freight transport is sermons. Sermons are the least restrictive type of measures since they do not force or push any behavior, but they rather suggest or recommend a specific behavior. Despite being less vigorous, these "soft" measures aiming for consciousness and understanding are rated as very important by the logistics companies (Pfoser, in press). The sermons category includes awareness raising activities as well as education and training.

Awareness building measures are relevant for all three types of sustainable freight transport. In context of horizontal collaboration, awareness for the positive effects of commonly operating transport and sharing logistics resources with partners must be in place (Plasch et al., 2021). Many stakeholders are hesitant to collaborate because they do not fully trust each other and refuse data exchange (Kurapati et al., 2018). A mental shift is needed for logistics companies to accept new types of collaborative transport (Pfoser et al., in press). Trust building measures are suitable to induce such a mental shift as they break up competitive thinking and suspicion among partners (Plasch et al., 2021). To promote multimodal freight transport, awareness building measures are also needed. Awareness raising campaigns (e.g. roadshows presenting successful business cases) should induce a mental shift in a way that logistics companies (especially shippers as "customers" of transport) start to regard multimodality as a viable transport option (Pfoser, in press). Importantly, awareness raising also includes managing customers' expectations: Shippers are most often used to the fact that goods arrive within a short period of time, and for that reason many shippers dramatically reduce their stocks. This behavior makes it difficult to implement multimodal solutions, as these solutions need some lead time and are rather suited for large cargo volumes put into interim storage. Shippers must accept the need to plan ahead and allow for interim stocks to facilitate multimodal transport (Pfoser, in press). Finally, awareness must also be raised for LNG as alternative truck fuel. Information campaigns and the demonstration of this technology may encourage users to invest in LNG vehicles (Pfoser et al., 2018d). LNG roadshows allow visitors to test the latest LNG truck technology. Within these events, visitors are allowed to drive LNG trucks, and they also gain an understanding of operational and maintenance issues related to this alternative fuel. This helps to reduce their concerns as they obtain practical insights and get in touch with the new technology (Pfoser et al., 2018d).

Education and training measures aim to raise knowledge of sustainable freight transport and provide logistics companies with experience of new technologies and services they might not have used before (Pfoser, in press). This is of particular importance for the shift and improve strategies which both involve special equipment and operations that might be new for the logistics companies. For example, using LNG as an alternative fuel requires the handling of a cryogenic liquid, which might deter fleet operators to switch to LNG trucks (Anderhofstadt and Spinler, 2019). In fact, the extremely low temperature of LNG constitutes a hazard for humans and materials that get in contact with it (Aneziris *et al.*, 2020). LNG fueling and storage also involve the risk of fires or explosions (Vanem *et al.*, 2008). These hazards can however be avoided through proper training of the employees handling LNG. For example, driver training familiarizes truck drivers with the operation of LNG fueled trucks. These measures address logistics companies' need for safety in transport (Pfoser *et al.*, 2016a) and popularize LNG as viable fuel option. Also in the field of multimodal transport education and training can be useful, for example to teach operators how to perform multimodal transport efficiently, but also for example to increase knowledge on which funding schemes exist to receive financial support (Pfoser, in press; Pfoser *et al.*, 2020).

6.3.5 Theoretical Support for the Identified Policy Measures

Based on the theoretical background presented in Subchapter 6.1, theoretical support can be provided for the identified policy measures. Figure 6.5 gives an overview of the theoretical implications that result for the identified policy measures using the theories introduced in Subchapter 6.1.

The use of monetary incentives to promote sustainable freight transport is supported by transaction cost economics. TCE teaches us that companies seek to reduce their transaction costs (Williamson, 1981). If the implementation of sustainable freight transport is subsidized, companies will incur reduced expenses and will be therefore encouraged to introduce sustainable strategies.

The resource-based view explains why infrastructure development and the adaptation of the legal framework are suitable to promote sustainable freight transport. According to RBV, resources are crucial to gain a competitive advantage (Barney, 1991). The natural resource-based view teaches us that pro-environmental practices may constitute a competitive advantage (Hart, 1995). Indeed, many logistics companies see sustainable transport as an opportunity to distinguish themselves from competitors (Pfoser, in press). It is therefore recommended to provide them with the required resources they need for sustainable freight transport. The resources that are needed to implement sustainable strategies include, for example, refueling infrastructure or multimodal terminals. Notably, resources are not always physical, but they may also constitute intangible framework conditions, such as the legal framework for sustainable freight transport.

The institutional theory gives indications of how information and transparency can be created within the transport system. As stated above, it is very important for stakeholders that the performance of a transport system (e.g. multimodal network or PI network) is monitored. This ensures that performance remains at the desired level and outcomes are satisfactory. However, transparency will probably not be granted automatically. Institutional theory (DiMaggio and Powell, 1983; Scott, 1987) suggests that coercive pressure is a suitable measure to dictate information and transparency. Coercive pressure constitutes the formal or informal constraints that are put on organizations (DiMaggio and Powell, 1983). These constraints are imposed by third parties upon which the organizations are dependent on, for example the legal regulatory system (Oliver, 1991). If regulatory authorities stipulate the monitoring of transport performance, stakeholders will have to obey. This will be beneficial for the efficiency (and thus the acceptance) of sustainable freight transport systems. Beside coercive pressure, another element of institutional theory can be borrowed for the development of policy measures, namely mimetic pressure. Mimetic pressure means that companies imitate the behavior of other organizations to avoid falling behind the technology leaders in their industry (DiMaggio and Powell, 1983). This mimetic behavior implies that pilot projects and business cases of pioneering companies in sustainable freight transport should be disseminated extensively to create mimetic pressure for others to follow the early adopters. The dissemination of pilot cases can be realized by information campaigns, roadshows or other awareness raising activities.

Awareness raising activities are intended to influence stakeholders in a way that they demand sustainable freight transport from their transport providers. The rationale for awareness raising measures is rooted in stakeholder theory and agency theory, which both explain the importance of stakeholders' expectations for the realization of sustainable practices. Following stakeholder theory (Freeman, 1984; Donaldson and Preston, 1995), companies are prompted to implement sustainable strategies if their stakeholders exhibit environmental needs. Similarly, agency theory (Eisenhardt, 1989) assumes that if their principals require sustainable behavior, companies (as agents) are motivated to show environmental commitment. Due to the significant power of the stakeholders, it is advisable to set awareness raising measures which target the environmental consciousness of the stakeholders. As argued in Section 5.2.3, the transport customers are the most important stakeholders for logistics service providers. Awareness raising measures should therefore specifically target transport customers, but also all other stakeholders including the logistics companies themselves.

Theoretical support for education and training measures comes from the knowledge-based view. According to the knowledge-based view, knowledge is strategically the most important resource an organization may possess (Grant, 1996). Appropriate knowledge allows organizations to gain a competitive advantage. In view of sustainable freight transport, green intellectual capital is relevant to implement environmentally friendly transport services. Education and training measures are therefore required to create this green intellectual capital. Practical experience and knowledge will reduce reluctance towards sustainable freight transport (Lazuras *et al.*, 2011).

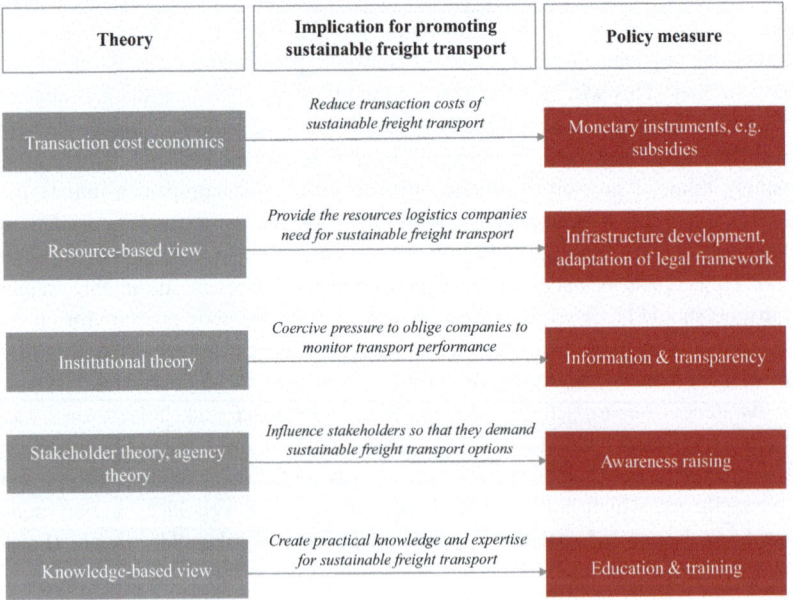

Figure 6.5 Theoretical support for identified policy measures

Conclusion

7.1 Synthesis of Results

This research uses an intense stakeholder dialogue with logistics companies to investigate the determinants of sustainable freight transport acceptance and identify user-centric policy measures to promote sustainable freight transport. A comparison of the determinants of acceptance and the suggested policy measures shows that each policy measure addresses a determinant of acceptance. Table 7.1 juxtaposes the determinants of acceptance and the policy measures and gives the underlying theoretical support as argued in Section 6.3.5.

Table 7.1 Comparison of determinants of acceptance and policy measures for sustainable freight transport

Determinant of acceptance	Policy measure	Theoretical support
Profitability	Monetary instruments	Transaction cost economics
Customer demand	Awareness raising, education & training	Stakeholder theory, agency theory, knowledge-based view
Availability of infrastructure	Infrastructure development	Resource-based view
Organizational efforts	Stipulate information & transparency	Institutional theory
Legal framework	Adaptation of legal framework	Resource-based view

LSPs' need for profitability can be addressed by monetary instruments such as the internalization of external costs or subsidies. These instruments will reduce the initial cost for establishing sustainable freight transport which will motivate

© The Author(s) 2022
S. Pfoser, *Decarbonizing Freight Transport*,
https://doi.org/10.1007/978-3-658-37103-6_7

companies to try and test sustainable practices. In the medium and long term, the costs for realizing the sustainable practices will decline automatically due to the market uptake of these practices and funding will not be required anymore.

Customer demand is an important driver for LSPs' acceptance to implement sustainable freight transport strategies. Customers' demand for sustainable freight transport can be evoked by awareness raising measures which create consciousness and a positive attitude towards sustainable practices. Managers buying transport services from LSPs must be aware that their buying decision has an enormous impact on the sustainable development of the transport system. This study revealed that hardly any LSP offers sustainable options without being requested to do so. This holds true for all three pillars of sustainable transport— avoid, shift as well as improve. During the empirical investigations it turned out that none of the sustainable strategies under study in this thesis would be established without customers (i.e. shippers) asking for environmentally friendly transport. Awareness raising is therefore a highly important instrument.

A policy measure that is related to awareness raising is education & training. Both, awareness raising and education & training target the creation of knowledge. While awareness raising creates theoretical knowledge and consciousness, education & training aims for practical knowledge and application-oriented skills to promote the implementation of sustainable practices. If LSPs have practical knowledge on how to operate sustainable transport, customers are encouraged to demand sustainable transport from them because they trust in the capabilities of the LSPs.

A basic prerequisite to realize sustainable freight transport (and thus a fundamental determinant of its acceptance) is the presence of the required infrastructure. In many cases, the implementation of sustainable practices is hampered simply because the infrastructure is missing. Policy should therefore accelerate the development of appropriate infrastructure and equipment. For example, they can fund the construction of infrastructure and announce public tenders for that purpose. This ensures that the resources required for sustainable freight transport are available.

Organizational efforts have been identified as another determinant of sustainable freight transport acceptance. If LSPs perceive it as complex to introduce sustainable practices, they will hesitate to do so. It turned out that many stakeholders perceive sustainable freight transport markets as non-transparent and difficult to enter. To reduce the perceived complexity, information and transparency about the organization, operation and performance of sustainable freight transport need to be provided. This transparency needs to be dictated by public authorities because transport providers will most probably not supply the required information on a voluntary basis.

Finally, the legal framework determines the acceptance of sustainable freight transport. Legal conditions can favor sustainable practices, e.g. they may give special permissions and preferential treatment to sustainable freight transport. As an example, truck transports within multimodal operations may be privileged by the granting of higher weight permissions. Another example is that LNG trucks are sometimes allowed to enter low-emission zones in city centers. However, the legal framework can also prevent the dissemination of sustainable freight strategies, for example in the case of cumbersome admission procedures. Policy measures should therefore target the creation of favorable legal framework conditions for logistics companies to introduce sustainable freight transport.

The preceding explanations in Subchapter 6.2 showed the existence of severe market failures in the sustainable freight transport market. It was demonstrated that due to these market failures, LSPs currently do not have an incentive for introducing sustainable freight strategies. For example, LSPs are reluctant to use sustainable practices because they do not (exclusively) benefit from the positive effects of introducing sustainable freight transport. This problem is known as the tragedy of the commons. Some LSPs also feel that there is no need for them to apply sustainable strategies because others might care for the environmental problems and shoulder this responsibility (free-rider behavior). Another problem is that there is imperfect information, such that many stakeholders do not possess the appropriate knowledge about sustainable freight transport. Finally, the existence of externalities hampers sustainable freight transport because the costs of environmental pollution are not reflected in transport prices (Figure 7.1).

The identified policy measures are able to minimize some of the market failures that currently exist in the sustainable freight transport market. For example, awareness raising measures can be used to create consciousness for common goods and prevent companies from exploiting these common resources such as air quality. The originator of the tragedy of commons, Garrett Hardin (1968), mentioned that there is no technical solution to overcome the economic problem of resource depletion. Instead, Hardin (1968, p. 1243) suggested that "a fundamental extension of morality" would be necessary to address the tragedy of commons. In fact, it has been proposed that sustainability problems should be framed as moral scarcity issue and not only as resource scarcity issue (Brown et al., 2019). Thus, moral norms need to be developed to fight collective exploitation of common goods. Awareness raising measures are able to deliver moral norms and communicate ethic principles of sustainability.

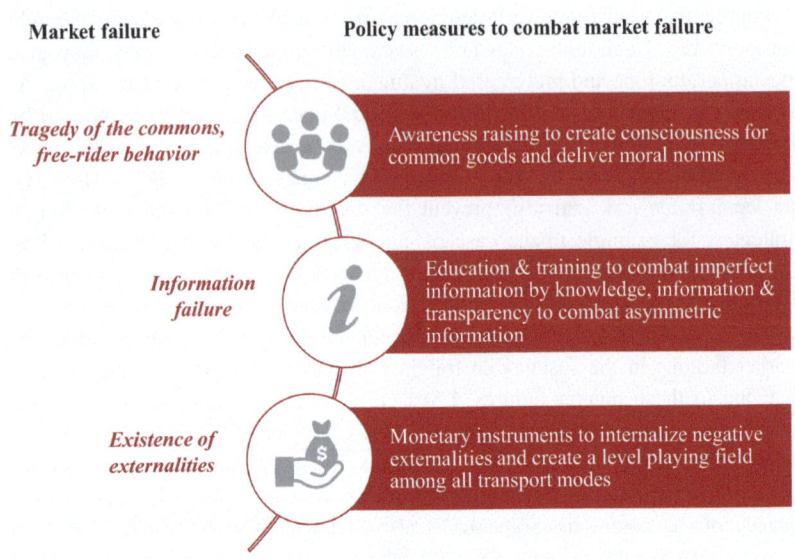

Market failure   **Policy measures to combat market failure**

Tragedy of the commons,
free-rider behavior

Awareness raising to create consciousness for
common goods and deliver moral norms

Information
failure

Education & training to combat imperfect
information by knowledge, information &
transparency to combat asymmetric
information

Existence of
externalities

Monetary instruments to internalize negative
externalities and create a level playing field
among all transport modes

Figure 7.1   Comparison of market failures and policy measures

To resolve the information failure that currently dominates sustainable freight transport, education and training is an appropriate measure. Education and training creates knowledge and thus removes imperfect information. Having better information and expertise in the field of sustainable freight transport will support LSPs to introduce environmentally friendly practices. Another information failure in sustainable freight transport markets is asymmetric information. Asymmetric information exists because some parties have better information on sustainable freight transport than other parties. This problem can be addressed by stipulating information and transparency for all players in the market. For example, shippers should have access to all required information on multimodal transport, e.g. service providers, costs, timetables, performance parameters, etc.

Finally, the existence of negative externalities can be prevented by using monetary instruments which aim to internalize external costs. Monetary instruments enforce the "polluter pays principle" and thus charge the causing of negative externalities. This creates a level playing field among all transport modes because external costs become part of the decision makers' choice process. At the moment, only direct costs such as operational costs, taxes or travel time opportunity cost are considered within the selection of a transport service (Márquez and Cantillo, 2013). The external costs (which are currently borne by society) are not adequately reflected in transport prices. The price of sustainable freight transport is therefore too high and must be altered by monetary instruments (emission charging, taxes, etc.).

7.2 Responses to the Research Questions

Based on the findings of this thesis, the research questions can be answered as follows. The first research question (which sustainable freight transport strategies exist to reduce the negative environmental impact of freight transport?) is answered by introducing the ASI framework (Chapter 4). The ASI framework is a well-known approach to classify strategies for sustainable freight transport. According to the ASI approach, there exist three main strategies to decarbonize freight transport, each of which represents a pillar of the framework: to avoid transport, to shift transport, and to improve transport (Figure 7.2). The papers of this thesis refer to three particular strategies, each of which addresses one of the three aforementioned pillars. Plasch *et al.* (2021) discuss horizontal collaboration in a PI network (avoid pillar), Pfoser (in press) elucidates multimodal freight transport (shift pillar) and Pfoser *et al.* (2018d) / Pfoser *et al.* (2016a) address LNG as an alternative fuel (improve pillar). It has been shown that all of these strategies are suitable and highly promising to reduce the negative environmental impact of freight transport, though their approach on how to achieve this goal is quite different. Horizontal collaboration has the potential to better utilize transport resources and reduce empty runs, and thereby reduce the environmental burden of transport. Multimodal freight transport is the combined use of multiple transport modes in a way such that the strengths of each mode can be utilized and the weaknesses can be compensated by the other mode(s). In this sense, multimodality creates better conditions for the use of sustainable transport modes, such as railways or waterways. And finally, LNG is at present the only viable alternative fuel for heavy-duty vehicles and long-haul transports. The technology for LNG is mature and readily available on the market, while other alternative fuels are still in a stage of development.

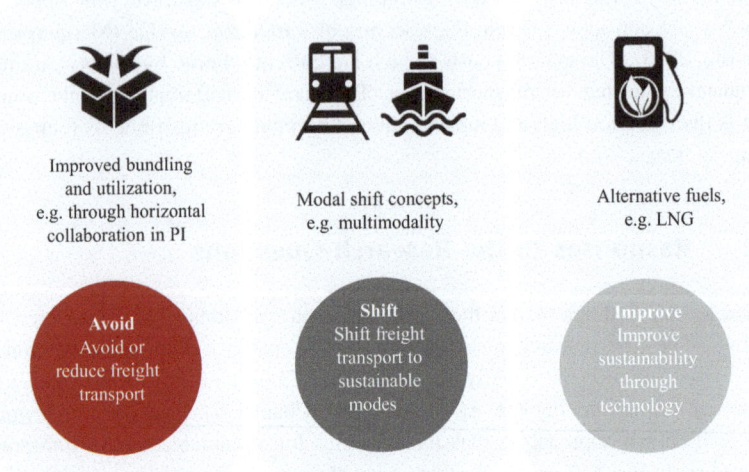

Figure 7.2 Overview of sustainable freight transport strategies

Though European politics shows strong commitment for all of the three strategies presented in Figure 7.2, they have not succeeded so far in promoting the acceptance and use of these strategies. Therefore, the second research question is framed as follows: Which determinants influence the acceptance of sustainable freight transport strategies?. Theoretical support for answering the second research questions comes from the technology acceptance model. The technology acceptance model (Davis, 1989) is a widely used theory to explain why decision makers adopt a specific technology or behavior. TAM postulates that two main determinants influence acceptance: the perceived usefulness and the perceived ease of use. The sub research questions regarding the acceptance of PI, multimodality and LNG (RQ 2.1–RQ 2.3) were answered by providing the individual determinants for these transport strategies (Table 5.2). Plasch *et al.* (2021) describe the motives to collaborate in a PI network, which are used to derive knowledge on the determinants of PI acceptance (RQ 2.1). Pfoser (in press) elaborates on the barriers to multimodality, which are used to derive the determinants of multimodality acceptance (RQ 2.2). Finally, Pfoser *et al.* (2018d) and Pfoser *et al.* (2016a) reveal the determinants of LNG acceptance (RQ 2.3). The individual determinants elaborated for each strategy were compared in Chapter 5 to derive overarching determinants of sustainable freight transport acceptance. Five main determinants were identified which influence the acceptance of avoid, shift and improve strategies (Figure 7.3). These determinants are profitability and customer demand (both of which refer to usability), as well as availability of infrastructure, organizational efforts and legal framework (which refer to the ease of using sustainable freight transport). These five determinants present the answer to the second research question.

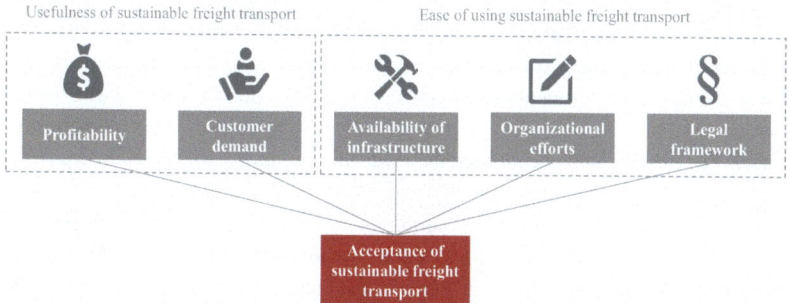

Figure 7.3 Determinants of sustainable freight transport acceptance

The third research question in this thesis examines which market failures occur in the area of sustainable freight transport and currently distort the acceptance of sustainable strategies (RQ 3). According to neoclassical welfare economics, the presence of market failures justifies the use of policy instruments to intervene in the markets (Al-Saleh and Mahroum, 2015). Four types of market failures were identified in Chapter 6.2, namely the tragedy of commons, the existence of externalities, information failure and free-rider behavior. The policy measures developed in the thesis should address and solve these market failures.

The fourth and final research question in this thesis is dedicated to the development of user-centric policy measures. Organizational theories were used as theoretical foundation to explain the mechanisms which drive transport users to adopt sustainable practices. These theories reveal that three main dimensions support the adoption of sustainable freight transport, namely (1) organizational obligations, (2) organizational capabilities and (3) organizational functioning. It can be concluded that policy measures should address these three dimensions to set mechanisms which effectively promote sustainable practices.

Based on a user-centric approach involving numerous LSPs, concrete suggestions for policy measures were developed. The sub research questions regarding policy measures to promote the PI, multimodality and LNG (RQ 4.1– RQ 4.3) were answered by providing individual policy measures for these three transport strategies (Table 6.2). Plasch *et al.* (2021) describe the success factors to collaborate in a PI network, which are used to derive policy measures for PI (RQ 4.1). Pfoser (in press) develops policy measures to promote multimodality (RQ 4.2). Finally, Pfoser *et al.* (2018d) and Pfoser *et al.* (2016a) suggest policy measures to foster LNG (RQ 4.3). The individual policy measures elaborated for each strategy were compared in Chapter 6 to derive overarching policy measures to promote sustainable freight transport. Due to the user-centric approach, it appeared that the common sticks-carrots-sermons classification previously used to categorize policy measures does not meet transport users' needs. Instead, a new typology is suggested, namely carrots-means-sermons. This typology provides an answer for the fourth research question (which policy measures promote the implementation of sustainable freight transport strategies?): on the one hand, monetary instruments ("carrots") may push environmental practices. On the other hand, the provision of basic infrastructure and framework conditions ("means") is an important impetus to implement sustainable strategies. Infrastructure development, information & transparency and the adaptation of the legal framework constitute means. Finally, the third category of policy instruments aims to create consciousness, knowledge and understanding to promote sustainable freight transport ("sermons"). Sermons are the least restrictive type of policy measures since they do not force or push any behavior, but rather suggest or recommend a specific behavior. Activities for awareness raising and education & training fall within this type of policy measure.

7.3   Contributions to the Domain of Sustainable Freight Transport

This thesis closes several research gaps and thereby makes theoretical as well as practical contributions to the domain of sustainable freight transport. The first research gap is the lack of a common definition of the construct acceptance in context of sustainable freight transport, which leads to an ambiguous use of this construct. Second, sustainable freight transport strategies have been previously studied in an isolated manner, whereas a holistic contemplation would lead to a more comprehensive strategy towards their introduction. Another research gap is the theoretical dearth that exists in green SCM. A topic which is absolutely under researched is the market failures that occur in the sustainable freight transport market. From a managerial perspective, there is a lack of research studies which incorporate a user-centric view to develop policy measures. This leads to the introduction of policy measures which do not meet the needs of transport users (i.e. logistics companies). This calls for a redesign of the common sticks-carrots-sermons typology to classify policy measures, since this typology fails to take users' needs into account.

Resulting from the aforementioned research gaps that were tackled in the thesis, there are four theoretical and two practical contributions to the domain of sustainable freight transport. These contributions will be presented hereafter.

Theoretical contribution 1: Setting a concise definition of acceptance in context of sustainable freight transport
A variety of definitions of the construct acceptance have been developed in the recent literature comprising different suggestions of how to describe users' acceptance of innovations or new technologies. This variety of definitions bears the risk of misinterpreting the results from different studies due to a missing common perception of the construct acceptance (Adell *et al.*, 2018). For instance, some studies refer to acceptance if users perceive an innovation as useful, other studies require the actual use of innovations for acceptance to take place. To eliminate this confusion, this thesis developed a concise definition of acceptance in the context of sustainable freight transport. The definition developed in Subchapter 2.1 emphasizes the need for using (or at least being willing to use) sustainable freight transport strategies to realize their intended benefits (i.e. decarbonizing freight transport). For acceptance to take place it is not enough to appreciate the usefulness of a strategy, instead there must be a clear willingness to implement the strategy, otherwise the positive effects of sustainable transport will not materialize. The definition also focuses on the logistics companies' perspective to account for the transport users' subjective judgment of sustainable freight transport strategies and logistics companies' expected gains from implementing these strategies. This fits with the overall user-oriented focus of this thesis, which brings transport users to the fore. To summarize, it is important to understand that acceptance is based on the transport users' judgment of an innovation or a new technology such as sustainable transport strategies. It is therefore necessary that users recognize the benefits or gains of using the innovation.

Theoretical contribution 2: Holistic view of different approaches to reduce carbon footprint of freight transport
In this thesis, the topic of sustainable freight transport is viewed from a holistic perspective. The study allows for the in-depth comparison of three different, heterogeneous approaches to reduce the environmental impact of freight transport. These three approaches are (1) to avoid transport (2) to shift transport and (3) to

improve transport (ASI framework). Existing studies only refer to one individual strategy limited to reducing the carbon footprint of transport, for example a specific transport concept such as combined transport only, or a specific technology such as a particular alternative powertrain only. There are hardly any studies which refer to different approaches and compare them. On the contrary, this study simultaneously examines avoid, shift and reduce strategies which allows the contextualization and juxtaposition of the characteristics and specificities of these three different approaches. Based on this holistic view, higher-level implications for the realization of the approaches can be derived and interrelationships can be identified. The holistic perspective allows the display of the transport sector as a whole system with various components that contribute to the overall goal, namely the decarbonization of freight transport. This thesis showed which overarching determinants affect the acceptance of sustainable freight transport in general. Based on that, some overarching policy measures were defined which promote the implementation of sustainable freight transport. Becoming acquainted with the higher-level determinants and the higher-level policy measures allows the gain of a better understanding for the basic direction in which the transport system has to move to become more sustainable. One individual strategy will not suffice to combat the environmental problems of the transport sector. The integrated and holistic view is therefore important to see the whole picture and form a comprehensive strategy for sustainable freight transport. This supports efficient policy making and promotes the decarbonization of freight transport.

Theoretical contribution 3: Developing a theoretical framework to explain the adoption of sustainable freight transport strategies
Recent literature underlines the theoretical dearth that exists in green SCM (Touboulic and Walker, 2015; Carter and Easton, 2011; Sarkis *et al.*, 2011). Sustainable freight transport can be considered a subdomain of green SCM (Putz *et al.*, 2018) and also lacks an appropriate theoretical underpinning. This thesis addresses the gap as it provides a comprehensive theoretical framework explaining the adoption of sustainable freight transport strategies (Subchapter 6.1). Well-established organizational theories are used to explain how logistics companies are encouraged to implement sustainable freight transport. Three dimensions of organizational existence are identified to substantiate why sustainable practices are introduced by LSPs. These three dimensions are organizational obligations, organizational capabilities and organizational functioning. Organizational obligations result from the logistics companies' responsibility towards their stakeholders (stakeholder theory, agency theory, institutional theory). If stakeholders (such as customers) expect green operations, LSPs are encouraged for sustainable freight

transport. Organizational capabilities determine the ability to introduce sustainable practices (resource-based view, knowledge-based view). If LSPs do not have the resources (physical resources or knowledge) to implement sustainable strategies, they will not be able to do so. Finally, organizational functioning, i.e. the companies' operational principles, influences the implementation of sustainable strategies. LSPs try to minimize transaction costs (transaction cost economics), thus they will be eager to introduce green practices if they see the possibility to reduce transaction costs and thus maintain their organizational functioning.

The categorization of organizational dimensions (obligations, capabilities and functioning) is new and provides a useful theoretical framework for future research in the domain of sustainable freight transport. The categorization encompasses all relevant areas of organizational existence. The proposed theoretical framework can be used to explain the occurrence of sustainable practices in green SCM and logistics. This will deepen the understanding of logistics companies' motives towards pro-environmental behavior and provides a starting point to define ways to encourage pro-environmental behavior.

Theoretical contribution 4: Explaining market failures which inhibit the implementation of sustainable freight transport
This is the first study that identifies different types of market failure to explain the reasons for the hesitant implementation of sustainable freight transport strategies. Hardly any studies refer to market failures as a rationale for the poor environmental performance of the logistics and transport sector. If at all, existing work only uses one individual type of market failure as an explanation. However, as shown in Subchapter 6.2, substantial market failures exist in the sustainable freight transport markets, and these market failures explain the rejection of sustainable strategies to a significant degree. The reason is that due to the existence of these market failures, logistics companies do not have an incentive to introduce sustainable freight transport. For example, logistics companies are not prevented from exploiting common resources (tragedy of the commons) and thus do not have an incentive to decarbonize their transport operations. Transport prices do not reflect environmental costs (existence of negative externalities), thus logistics companies are not encouraged to use sustainable transport. Additionally, many companies lack the required knowledge to introduce sustainable practices (imperfect information). As can be seen, the consideration of market failures allows insights into why the decarbonization of logistics is currently inhibited. Thereby, this thesis reveals important mechanisms and a new reasoning for the environmental problems of freight transport.

Practical contribution 1: User-centric view to promote the acceptance of sustainable freight transport

The users of sustainable freight transport are crucial players for the implementation of environmentally friendly transport systems. This thesis is one of the first studies which brings the users of sustainable freight transport to the fore as it analyzes the determinants of users' acceptance and collects users' suggestions for policy measures. Existing work strongly concentrates on the supply of sustainable freight transport and neglects the demand perspective. For example, studies on horizontal collaboration in a PI network predominantly deal with supply-related questions such as the design of PI containers to be used in the network or the development of decision support models to assist the operation of PI services (Plasch *et al.*, 2021). Similarly, studies on horizontal collaboration in a synchromodal network have also focused tremendously on the supply side, for example by developing ICT systems and planning models for synchromodality (Pfoser *et al.*, in press). The same problem persists within the literature on multimodal transport: a plethora of publications concentrates on multimodal transport planning, i.e. the design and optimization of multimodal transport chains (Agamez-Arias and Moyano-Fuentes, 2017). By contrast, there are only few studies which examine the demand for multimodal freight transport. Finally, also the literature on LNG as alternative truck fuel suffers from the same problem. A lot of technical studies exist covering supply-related topics such as the optimum fuel pressure of LNG vehicles, fuel tank systems, safety of storage facilities, and so on. Many publications also exist offering life-cycle analyses of GHG emissions. However, only a few studies refer to demand-related issues of LNG as an alternative fuel.

As illustrated above, the existing literature perfectly supports the supply of sustainable freight transport by developing knowledge about technology-related questions regarding the provision of sustainable freight transport (e.g. ICT systems or infrastructure such as terminals or refueling systems) or by providing planning models (e.g. for the transport service design). The supply-related studies are important to stimulate the provision of sustainable freight transport. However, it is equally important to understand the demand for sustainable freight transport, because without users' demand, sustainable strategies will not be realized in practice. Users' requirements and motives need to be considered in the process of advancing sustainable strategies to ensure their acceptance. Information on users' requirements and motives is essential to adequately address the needs of those who finally implement sustainable freight transport. However, the abundance of supply-related studies do not provide information on users' needs and demand. The present thesis contributes to this gap as it provides information on the determinants of users' sustainable freight transport acceptance. The thesis also presents policy measures which are from users' viewpoint appropriate to promote sustainable freight transport. These policy measures reflect the needs of those who use sustainable freight transport and therefore these measures have the potential to really initiate the decarbonization of freight transport.

Practical contribution 2: Extending the common environmental policy typology from the users' perspective

The commonly used typology to classify environmental policy measures is the threefold sticks-carrots-sermons approach (Subchapter 2.2). This thesis reveals that from transport users' perspective, the sticks-carrots-sermons typology falls short when applied to the field of sustainable freight transport. As illustrated in Subchapter 6.3, logistics companies do not favor the instrument of sticks (i.e. regulations and sanctions) to force sustainable practices. Instead, they suggest a new type of policy measure which is not covered by the previous sticks-carrots-sermons typology, namely means. The instrument of means involves the development of infrastructure and other framework conditions to support logistics companies with the introduction of sustainable freight transport. Means may constitute regulations (legal framework), but they are different from sticks as they do not force the target group to use the innovation. Means may also constitute economic instruments as infrastructure provision will be bound up with monetary investments. However, means differ from carrots as they do not make it cheaper or more expensive for the target group to use the innovation, but they make it possible to use the innovation.

Extending the existing threefold environmental policy typology by the category "means" is an important contribution for the domain of sustainable freight transport. Means (such as infrastructural development) have the potential to encourage logistics companies towards more sustainable behavior while at the same time maintaining the decision makers' freedom to choose and not to oblige them to adopt a specific behavior. The intention of means is to encourage potential users by changing the built environment (Mattauch *et al.*, 2016) or framework conditions. Means are a valuable complement to the original sticks, carrots and sermons instruments. The acceptance of means is expected to be high since it is a measure directly suggested by transport users. Policy makers should therefore consider means as a powerful instrument when seeking to promote sustainable freight transport.

7.4   Limitations, Further Research and Outlook

This thesis has several limitations that call for further research. First, the thesis claims to provide a holistic view of sustainable freight transport by juxtaposing different strategies that fall within different pillars of sustainable freight transport. However, within the scope of this thesis only three exemplary strategies were investigated, one for each pillar of the ASI model. Future research is needed to examine other strategies as well and ensure that they follow the same principles and lead to the same conclusions regarding the acceptance and policy measures for sustainable freight transport.

Second, the acceptance study is primarily based on qualitative research (interviews, focus groups). Qualitative research is limited to the results that emerge from the specific case companies under investigation. Although the case companies were selected deliberately to achieve a heterogeneous sample, it cannot be concluded without a doubt that the findings about sustainable freight transport acceptance are transferable to any logistics company in any industry. Further research could examine if the results also hold within other research settings, e.g. companies with different size, cultural context or organizational background.

Third, the thesis takes a user-centric perspective, which means that assessing the measures from the political perspective is not part of this study and should be covered by future research. The policy measures were developed within a qualitative and user-focused research process and reflect logistics companies' needs towards sustainable freight transport. To account for the political perspective, it will be necessary to evaluate the viability and potential effects of the suggested measures. It is another limitation of this thesis that the suggested strategies are viewed in an isolated manner. In practice, single policy measures are hardly ever used on their own. Instead, it is more common (and more efficient) to use a mixture of these (Glasbergen, 1992; Taylor et al., 2012). Further research should therefore also focus on the question which combination of the suggested policy measures is the best to promote sustainable freight transport. Special attention must also be paid to the problem of rebound effects. A rebound effect offsets the positive effects of a policy measure (e.g. sustainable freight transport strategy) due to changed customer behavior (Matos and Silva, 2011). For example, due to the promotion of alternative fuels for road vehicles the use of road transport may increase, which offsets the efficiency gains of alternative fuels. Potential rebound effects that may occur along with the proposed strategies must therefore be identified and evaluated.

Subchapter 6.2 outlined several market failures that occur in the sustainable freight transport market. This outline is only an initial attempt to capture the market failures that impede sustainable freight transport. Further research should aim for an in-depth econometric analysis of the mechanisms causing these market failures. The characteristics of sustainable freight transport markets must be studied in more detail to understand which problems hinder the decarbonization of logistics. The basic assumption of welfare economics should be proved for the context of sustainable freight transport. This will help to gain further insights into how to remove the barriers which currently inhibit sustainable freight transport.

The empirical investigation in this thesis revealed that customer relationships are an extremely important lever to facilitate sustainable freight transport. Nearly all logistics companies stated that they would implement sustainable practices if they are requested to do so by their customers. They argue that in the end, it is the customer who has to pay for the transport services. If the customer is willing to pay for sustainable transport, then the logistics companies would implement sustainable practices. This finding is substantiated by two popular theories, stakeholder theory (Freeman, 1984) and agency theory (Eisenhardt, 1989). Both theories hypothesize that organizations follow the external pressure and needs from their stakeholders or agents, which are for example their customers. Since customer demand for sustainable freight transport is one of the most powerful motivators for LSPs to decarbonize their transport operations, future actions must involve customers, i.e. shippers (Figure 7.4). This call is consistent with Eng-Larsson and Kohn (2012) who criticize that most research addresses the logistics' perspective and neglects the shippers' contextual viewpoints. Shippers must develop environmental awareness to drive their LSPs towards sustainable behavior. In general, environmental performance must become part of the freight transport and logistics procurement processes, which is currently not the case. The planning, tendering and contracting processes should consider environmental KPIs such as emission intensity. Currently, the transport price is the most decisive factor for transport customers in the logistics procurement process. In the future, the reduction in carbon foot print should be a relevant goal for shippers in their freight transport and logistics procurement.

As a final remark it should be noted that the sustainable freight transport strategies under study in this thesis (ASI strategies) reinforce each other and create synergetic effects when implemented together. Figure 7.5 illustrates some of these synergetic effects that occur between the individual strategies. For example, horizontal collaboration allows for the bundling of transportation flows which in turn facilitates multimodal transport (as multimodal transport requires large cargo volumes to utilize the higher capacities of sustainable transport modes). Similarly, horizontal collaboration may encourage the use of alternative fuels as risk sharing and asset sharing reduce the uncertainty that is bound up with new technologies

Figure 7.4 Transport
customers as relevant
decisions makers

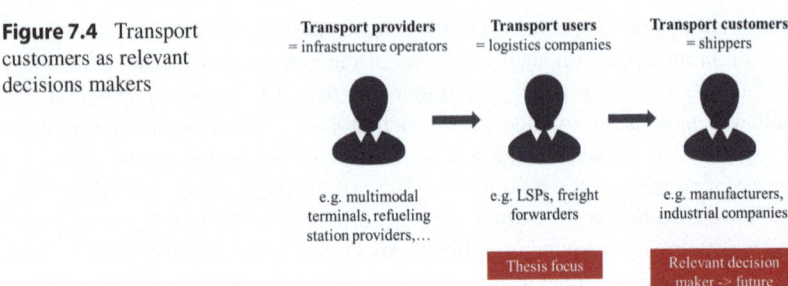

for logistics companies. Alternative fuels and multimodal transport also reinforce each other since alternative fuels make the first mile and last mile of multimodal operations greener and thereby make multimodal transport more competitive.

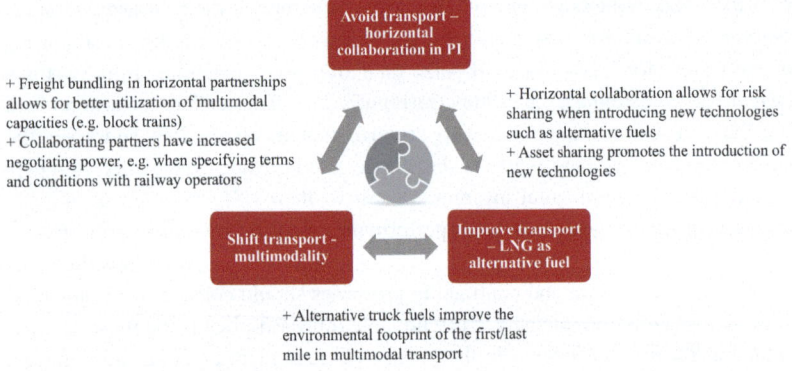

Figure 7.5   Synergetic effects of sustainable freight transport strategies

Due to the synergetic effects described above it is suggested that the ASI strategies should be implemented together and all of them should be promoted equally. This finding confirms the appropriateness of the holistic approach of this thesis, i.e. to regard all three ASI strategies simultaneously and compare the similarities concerning their determinants of acceptance and policy measures. Policy makers are advised to incorporate the synergetic effects and develop an integrated sustainable transport system where all three ASI pillars are implemented appropriately.

References

Abbassi, A., Alaoui, A.E.h. and Boukachour, J. (2019), "Robust optimisation of the intermodal freight transport problem: modeling and solving with an efficient hybrid approach", *Journal of Computational Science*, Vol. 30, pp. 127–142.

Adell, E., Várhelyi, A. and Nilsson, L. (2018), "The definition of acceptance and acceptability", in Regan, M.A., Stevens, A. and Horberry, T. (Eds.), *Driver acceptance of new technology: Theory, measurement and optimisation, Human factors in road and rail transport*, Ashgate Publishing Company, Burlington, VT, pp. 11–21.

Agamez-Arias, A.-M. and Moyano-Fuentes, J. (2017), "Intermodal transport in freight distribution. A literature review", *Transport Reviews*, Vol. 37 No. 6, pp. 782–807.

Aguilera-Caracuel, J., Hurtado-Torres, N.E. and Aragón-Correa, J.A. (2012), "Does international experience help firms to be green? A knowledge-based view of how international experience and organisational learning influence proactive environmental strategies", *International Business Review*, Vol. 21 No. 5, pp. 847–861.

Ajzen, I. (1985), "From intentions to actions: A theory of planned behavior", in Kuhland, J. and Beckman, J. (Eds.), *Action control*, Springer, pp. 11–39.

Ajzen, I. (1991), "The theory of planned behavior", *Organizational Behavior and Human Decision Processes*, Vol. 50 No. 2, pp. 179–211.

Ajzen, I. and Fishbein, M. (1980), *Understanding attitudes and predicting social behavior*, Pbk. ed., Prentice-Hall, Englewood Cliffs, N.J.

Alamia, A., Magnusson, I., Johnsson, F. and Thunman, H. (2016), "Well-to-wheel analysis of bio-methane via gasification, in heavy duty engines within the transport sector of the European Union", *Applied Energy*, Vol. 170, pp. 445–454.

Alharbi, S. and Drew, S. (2014), "Using the technology acceptance model in understanding academics' behavioural intention to use learning management systems", *International Journal of Advanced Computer Science and Applications*, Vol. 5 No. 1, pp. 143–155.

Al-Saleh, Y. and Mahroum, S. (2015), "A critical review of the interplay between policy instruments and business models: greening the built environment a case in point", *Journal of Cleaner Production*, Vol. 109, pp. 260–270.

Ambra, T., Caris, A. and Macharis, C. (2019), "Towards freight transport system unification: reviewing and combining the advancements in the physical internet and synchromodal transport research", *International Journal of Production Research*, Vol. 57 No. 6, pp. 1606–1623.

© The Editor(s) (if applicable) and The Author(s) 2022
S. Pfoser, *Decarbonizing Freight Transport*,
https://doi.org/10.1007/978-3-658-37103-6

Ambra, T., Meers, D., Caris, A. and Macharis, C. (2017), "Inducing a new paradigm shift. A different take on synchromodal transport modelling", *Proceedings of the 4th International Physical Internet Conference*, pp. 4–18.

Anderhofstadt, B. and Spinler, S. (2019), "Factors affecting the purchasing decision and operation of alternative fuel-powered heavy-duty trucks in Germany—A Delphi study", *Transportation Research Part D: Transport and Environment*, Vol. 73, pp. 87–107.

Aneziris, O., Koromila, I. and Nivolianitou, Z. (2020), "A systematic literature review on LNG safety at ports", *Safety Science*, Vol. 124, p. 104595.

Arencibia, A.I., Feo-Valero, M., García-Menéndez, L. and Román, C. (2015), "Modelling mode choice for freight transport using advanced choice experiments", *Transportation Research Part A: Policy and Practice*, Vol. 75, pp. 252–267.

Arteconi, A., Brandoni, C., Evangelista, D. and Polonara, F. (2010), "Life-cycle greenhouse gas analysis of LNG as a heavy vehicle fuel in Europe", *Applied Energy*, Vol. 87 No. 6, pp. 2005–2013.

Arteconi, A. and Polonara, F. (2013), "LNG as vehicle fuel and the problem of supply: The Italian case study", *Energy Policy*, Vol. 62, pp. 503–512.

Ausserer, K. and Risser, R. (2005), "Intelligent transport systems and services. Chances and risks", *Proceedings of the 18th ICTCT workshop*, pp. 1–9.

Bakker, S., Zuidgeest, M., Coninck, H. de and Huizenga, C. (2014), "Transport, development and climate change mitigation: towards an integrated approach", *Transport Reviews*, Vol. 34 No. 3, pp. 335–355.

Barari, S., Agarwal, G., Zhang, W.C., Mahanty, B. and Tiwari, M.K. (2012), "A decision framework for the analysis of green supply chain contracts: An evolutionary game approach", *Expert systems with applications*, Vol. 39 No. 3, pp. 2965–2976.

Barney, J. (1991), "Firm resources and sustained competitive advantage", *Journal of Management*, Vol. 17 No. 1, pp. 99–120.

Barratt, M. (2004), "Understanding the meaning of collaboration in the supply chain", *Supply Chain Management: An International Journal*, Vol. 9 No. 1, pp. 30–42.

Battini, D., Boysen, N. and Emde, S. (2013), "Just-in-Time supermarkets for part supply in the automobile industry", *Journal of Management Control*, Vol. 24 No. 2, pp. 209–217.

Bax, C. (2011), *Policy instruments for managing EU road safety targets: carrots, sticks or sermons?*, R-2011-15, Leidschendam, The Netherlands.

Behdani, B., Fan, Y., Wiegmans, B. and Zuidwijk, R. (2016), "Multimodal schedule design for synchromodal freight transport systems", *European Journal of Transport and Infrastructure Research*, Vol. 16 No. 3, pp. 424–444.

Berrone, P. and Gomez-Mejia, L.R. (2009), "Environmental performance and executive compensation: An integrated agency-institutional perspective", *Academy of Management Journal*, Vol. 52 No. 1, pp. 103–126.

Bongardt, D., Stiller, L., Swart, A. and Wagner, A. (2019), *Sustainable Urban Transport: Avoid-Shift-Improve (A-S-I)*, Eschborn.

Bretzke, W.-R. (2011), "Sustainable logistics: In search of solutions for a challenging new problem", *Logistics Research*, Vol. 3 No. 4, pp. 179–189.

Bretzke, W.-R. (2014), *Nachhaltige Logistik: Zukunftsfähige Netzwerk-und Prozessmodelle*, Springer-Verlag.

Brookhuis, K.A., Waard, D. de and Janssen, W.H. (2019), "Behavioural impacts of advanced driver assistance systems–an overview", *European Journal of Transport and Infrastructure Research*, Vol. 1 No. 3.

Brown, K., Adger, W.N. and Cinner, J.E. (2019), "Moving climate change beyond the tragedy of the commons", *Global Environmental Change*, Vol. 54, pp. 61–63.

Buijs, P., Alvarez, J.A.L., Veenstra, M. and Roodbergen, K.J. (2016), "Improved collaborative transport planning at Dutch Logistics Service Provider Fritom", *Interfaces*, Vol. 46 No. 2, pp. 119–132.

Burger, J. and Gochfeld, M. (1998), "The tragedy of the commons 30 years later", *Environment: Science and Policy for Sustainable Development*, Vol. 40 No. 10, pp. 4–13.

Caniëls, M.C., Gehrsitz, M.H. and Semeijn, J. (2013), "Participation of suppliers in greening supply chains: An empirical analysis of German automotive suppliers", *Journal of Purchasing and Supply Management*, Vol. 19 No. 3, pp. 134–143.

Caplice, C. (2007), "Electronic markets for truckload transportation", *Production and Operations Management*, Vol. 16 No. 4, pp. 423–436.

Carter, C.R. and Easton, L.P. (2011), "Sustainable supply chain management: evolution and future directions", *International Journal of Physical Distribution & Logistics Management*, Vol. 41 No. 1, pp. 46–62.

Carter, C.R. and Rogers, D.S. (2008), "A framework of sustainable supply chain management: moving toward new theory", *International Journal of Physical Distribution & Logistics Management*.

Castritius, S.-M., Hecht, H., Möller, J., Dietz, C.J., Schubert, P., Bernhard, C., Morvilius, S., Haas, C.T. and Hammer, S. (2020), "Acceptance of truck platooning by professional drivers on German highways. A mixed methods approach", *Applied Ergonomics*, Vol. 85, pp. 1–10.

Chaabane, A., Ramudhin, A. and Paquet, M. (2012), "Design of sustainable supply chains under the emission trading scheme", *International Journal of Production Economics*, Vol. 135 No. 1, pp. 37–49.

Chang, D., Rhee, T., Nam, K., Chang, K., Lee, D. and Jeong, S. (2008), "A study on availability and safety of new propulsion systems for LNG carriers", *Reliability Engineering & System Safety*, Vol. 93 No. 12, pp. 1877–1885.

Chargui, T., Bekrar, A., Reghioui, M. and Trentesaux, D. (2020), "Proposal of a multi-agent model for the sustainable truck scheduling and containers grouping problem in a Road-Rail physical internet hub", *International Journal of Production Research*, Vol. 58 No. 18, pp. 1–25.

Chen, C., Xu, X. and Arpan, L. (2017), "Between the technology acceptance model and sustainable energy technology acceptance model: Investigating smart meter acceptance in the United States", *Energy Research & Social Science*, Vol. 25, pp. 93–104.

Chen, C.-F. and Chao, W.-H. (2011), "Habitual or reasoned? Using the theory of planned behavior, technology acceptance model, and habit to examine switching intentions toward public transit", *Transportation Research Part F: Traffic Psychology and Behaviour*, Vol. 14 No. 2, pp. 128–137.

Chen, C.-H., Wang, C.-L. and Chen, P.-Y. (2018), "Performance evaluation of the Service Industry Innovation Research program: The application of a means-end chain", *Technology in Society*, Vol. 54, pp. 111–119.

Chen, Q.-S., Wegrzyn, J. and Prasad, V. (2004), "Analysis of temperature and pressure changes in liquefied natural gas (LNG) cryogenic tanks", *Cryogenics*, Vol. 44 No. 10, pp. 701–709.

Chismar, W.G. and Wiley-Patton, S. (2003), "Does the extended technology acceptance model apply to physicians", in *Proceedings of the 36th Annual Hawaii International Conference on System Sciences, 2003*, IEEE, 1–8.

Chu, Z., Wang, L. and Lai, F. (2019), "Customer pressure and green innovations at third party logistics providers in China", *The International Journal of Logistics Management*, Vol. 30 No. 1, pp. 57–75.

Chun, Z. (2010), "Fire Control Design Scheme of LNG Vehicle Filling Station", *Gas & Heat*, Vol. 1.

Ciprés, C. and de la Cruz, M. Teresa (2019), "The Physical Internet from shippers perspective", in Müller, B. and Meyer, G. (Eds.), *Towards user-centric transport in Europe: Challenges, solutions and collaborations*, Springer International Publishing, Cham, pp. 203–221.

Clausen, U. and Voll, R. (2013), "A comparison of North American and European railway systems", *European Transport Research Review*, Vol. 5 No. 3, pp. 129–133.

Cordeiro, J.J. and Sarkis, J. (2008), "Does explicit contracting effectively link CEO compensation to environmental performance?", *Business Strategy and the Environment*, Vol. 17 No. 5, pp. 304–317.

Cruijssen, F., Cools, M. and Dullaert, W. (2007), "Horizontal cooperation in logistics: opportunities and impediments", *Transportation Research Part E: Logistics and Transportation Review*, Vol. 43 No. 2, pp. 129–142.

Dai, B. and Chen, H. (2012), "Profit allocation mechanisms for carrier collaboration in pickup and delivery service", *Computers & Industrial Engineering*, Vol. 62 No. 2, pp. 633–643.

Dalal-Clayton, B. and Bass, S. (2002), *Sustainable development strategies*, 1st ed., Earthscan Publications, London.

Dalkmann, H. and Brannigan, C. (2014), *Urban transport and climate change*, Bonn, Eschborn.

Dalla Chiara, B., Deflorio, F.P. and Spione, D. (2008), "The rolling road between the Italian and French Alps: modeling the modal split", *Transportation Research Part E: Logistics and Transportation Review*, Vol. 44 No. 6, pp. 1162–1174.

Daly, H.E. (1990), "Toward some operational principles of sustainable development", *Ecological Economics*, Vol. 2 No. 1, pp. 1–6.

Danielis, R. and Rotaris, L. (2014), "The rolling motorway as an alternative to door-to-door unimodal road transport: lessons from the Trieste-Chop project", *Zeitschrift fuer Verkehrswissenschaft*, Vol. 85 No. 1, pp. 1–31.

Darvish, M., Larrain, H. and Coelho, L.C. (2016), "A dynamic multi-plant lot-sizing and distribution problem", *International Journal of Production Research*, Vol. 54 No. 22, pp. 6707–6717.

Davis, F.D. (1989), "Perceived usefulness, perceived ease of use, and user acceptance of information technology", *MIS Quarterly*, Vol. 13, pp. 319–339.

Demir, E., Huang, Y., Scholts, S. and van Woensel, T. (2015), "A selected review on the negative externalities of the freight transportation: modeling and pricing", *Transportation Research Part E: Logistics and Transportation Review*, Vol. 77, pp. 95–114.

Deng, P., Liang, J., Wu, Y. and Li, T. (2019), "Dynamic boil-off characterization for discharge process of LNG vehicle tank", *Energy*, Vol. 186, p. 115813.

Deutscher Bundestag (1994), *Zweiter Bericht der Enquete-Kommission "Schutz der Erdatmosphäre" zum Thema Mobilität und Klima—Wege zu einer klimaverträglichen Verkehrspolitik.*

Dillon, A. and Morris, M.G. (1996), "User acceptance of new information technology: Theories and models", in Williams, M. (Ed.), *Annual Review of Information Science and Technology*, Medford, NJ: Information Today, pp. 3–32.

DiMaggio, P.J. and Powell, W.W. (1983), "The iron cage revisited: Institutional isomorphism and collective rationality in organizational fields", *American Sociological Review*, Vol. 48 No. 2, pp. 147–160.

Donaldson, T. and Preston, L.E. (1995), "The stakeholder theory of the corporation: Concepts, evidence, and implications", *Academy of Management Review*, Vol. 20 No. 1, pp. 65–91.

Duarte, A.E., Sarache, W.A. and Costa, Y.J. (2014), "A facility-location model for biofuel plants: Applications in the Colombian context", *Energy*, Vol. 72, pp. 476–483.

Dubey, R. and Bag, S. (2013), "Exploring the dimensions of sustainable practices an empirical study on Indian manufacturing firms", *International Journal of Operations and Quantitative Management*, Vol. 19 No. 2, pp. 123–146.

Dubey, R., Gunasekaran, A. and Papadopoulos, T. (2017), "Green supply chain management: theoretical framework and further research directions", *Benchmarking: An International Journal*, Vol. 24 No. 1, pp. 184–218.

Durbin, D.J. and Malardier-Jugroot, C. (2013), "Review of hydrogen storage techniques for on board vehicle applications", *International Journal of Hydrogen Energy*, Vol. 38 No. 34, pp. 14595–14617.

Eagly, A.H. and Chaiken, S. (1993), *The psychology of attitudes*, Harcourt Brace Jovanovich College Publishers.

ECMT (1998), *Report on the Current State of Combined Transport in Europe*, Paris.

Eisenhardt, K.M. (1989), "Agency theory: An assessment and review", *Academy of Management Review*, Vol. 14 No. 1, pp. 57–74.

Engel, K.H. and Saleska, S.R. (2005), "Subglobal regulation of the global commons: the case of climate change", *Ecology Law Quarterly*, Vol. 32 No. 2, pp. 183–233.

Engerer, H. and Horn, M. (2010), "Natural gas vehicles: An option for Europe", *Energy Policy*, Vol. 38 No. 2, pp. 1017–1029.

Eng-Larsson, F. and Kohn, C. (2012), "Modal shift for greener logistics—the shipper's perspective", *International Journal of Physical Distribution & Logistics Management*, Vol. 42 No. 1, pp. 36–59.

European Commission (2006), *Keep Europe moving: sustainable mobility for our continent: mid-term review of the European Commission's 2001 Transport White Paper*, COM(2006) 314 final.

European Commission (2011), *White Paper. Roadmap to a Single European Transport Area: Towards a Competitive and Resource Efficient Transport System*, COM(2011) 144 final, Brussels.

European Commission (2014), *Public consultation on Combined Transport: Report on the contributions received.*

European Commission (2019), *EU transport in figures: Statistical pocketbook 2019*, Bielot, Belgium.

European Environment Agency (2019a), "Freight transport volume and modal split within the EU", available at: https://www.eea.europa.eu/data-and-maps/daviz/freight-transport-volume-6#tab-chart_1 (accessed 17 October 2020).

European Environment Agency (2019b), "National emissions reported to the UNFCCC and to the EU Greenhouse Gas Monitoring Mechanism. DAT-13-en", available at: https://www.eea.europa.eu/data-and-maps/data/national-emissions-reported-to-the-unfccc-and-to-the-eu-greenhouse-gas-monitoring-mechanism-15 (accessed 21 May 2020).

Farrell, A.E., Keith, D.W. and Corbett, J.J. (2003), "A strategy for introducing hydrogen into transportation", *Energy Policy*, Vol. 31 No. 13, pp. 1357–1367.

Faysse, N. (2005), "Coping with the tragedy of the commons: Game structure and design of rules", *Journal of Economic Surveys*, Vol. 19 No. 2, pp. 239–261.

Fazili, M., Venkatadri, U., Cyrus, P. and Tajbakhsh, M. (2017), "Physical Internet, conventional and hybrid logistic systems: a routing optimisation-based comparison using the Eastern Canada road network case study", *International Journal of Production Research*, Vol. 55 No. 9, pp. 2703–2730.

Feldpausch-Jaegers, S., Lefort, N., Lange, M., Mozgovoy, A., Burmeister, F., Henel, M., Wehling, A., Schuhmann, E., Erler, R., Ruf, J., Köppel, W., Gerstein, D. and Brandes, F. (2016), *Potenzialanalyse LNG—Einsatz von LNG in der Mobilität, Schwerpunkte und Handlungsempfehlungen für die technische Umsetzung*, Essen.

Fischer, A., Nokhart, H., Olsen, H., Fagerholt, K., Rakke, J.G. and Stålhane, M. (2016), "Robust planning and disruption management in roll-on roll-off liner shipping", *Transportation Research Part E: Logistics and Transportation Review*, Vol. 91, pp. 51–67.

Fishbein, M. and Ajzen, I. (1975), *Belief, Attitude, Intention and Behavior: an Introduction to Theory and Research*, Addison-Wesley Pub. Co., Reading, Mass. Don Mills, Ontario, ON.

Fleury, S., Tom, A., Jamet, E. and Colas-Maheux, E. (2017), "What drives corporate car-sharing acceptance? A French case study", *Transportation Research Part F: Traffic Psychology and Behaviour*, Vol. 45, pp. 218–227.

Flodén, J., Bärthel, F. and Sorkina, E. (2017), "Transport buyers choice of transport service – A literature review of empirical results", *Research in Transportation Business & Management*, Vol. 23, pp. 35–45.

Freeman, R.E. (1984), *Strategic management: A stakeholder approach*, Pitman, Boston.

Freight Transport Association (2019), *Logistics Report 2019*, Kent, UK.

Fulton, L., Lah, O. and Cuenot, F. (2013), "Transport Pathways for Light Duty Vehicles: Towards a 2° Scenario", *Sustainability*, Vol. 5 No. 5, pp. 1863–1874.

Geerlings, H., Kuipers, B. and Zuidwijk, R. (2017), *Ports and Networks: Strategies, Operations and Perspectives*, Routledge.

Geldmacher, W., Just, V., Kopia, J. and Kompalla, A. (2017), "Development of a modified technology acceptance model for an innovative car sharing concept with self-driving cars", *Proceedings of BASIQ 2017 "New Trends in Sustainable Business and Consumption"*, pp. 269–276.

Ghaderi, H., Cahoon, S. and Nguyen, H.-O. (2016), "The role of intermodal terminals in the development of non-bulk rail freight market in Australia", *Case Studies on Transport Policy*, Vol. 4 No. 4, pp. 294–305.

Glasbergen, P. (1992), "Seven steps towards an instrumentation theory for environmental policy", *Policy & Politics*, Vol. 20 No. 3, pp. 191–200.

Gold, S., Seuring, S. and Beske, P. (2010), "Sustainable supply chain management and inter-organizational resources: a literature review", *Corporate Social Responsibility and Environmental Management*, Vol. 17 No. 4, 230–245.

Gondal, I.A. and Sahir, M.H. (2012), "Prospects of natural gas pipeline infrastructure in hydrogen transportation", *International Journal of Energy Research*, Vol. 36 No. 15, pp. 1338–1345.

Gontara, S., Boufaied, A. and Korbaa, O. (2018), "Routing the PI-containers in the Physical Internet using the PI-BGP protocol", Aqaba.

González, P., Sarkis, J. and Adenso-Díaz, B. (2008), "Environmental management system certification and its influence on corporate practices", *International Journal of Operations & Production Management*, Vol. 28 No. 11, pp. 1021–1041.

Grant, R.M. (1996), "Toward a knowledge-based theory of the firm", *Strategic Management Journal*, Vol. 17 No. S2, pp. 109–122.

Grazia Speranza, M. (2018), "Trends in transportation and logistics", *European Journal of Operational Research*, Vol. 264 No. 3, pp. 830–836.

Greene, S. and Lewis, A. (2019), *Global logistics emissions council framework for logistics emissions accounting and reporting*, Amsterdam.

Grisolía, J.M. and López del Pino, F. (2008), "Some new evidence in the determination of acceptability of urban transport pricing".

Guang Shi, V., Lenny Koh, S.C., Baldwin, J. and Cucchiella, F. (2012), "Natural resource based green supply chain management", *Supply Chain Management: An International Journal*, Vol. 17 No. 1, pp. 54–67.

Guglielminetti, P., Piccioni, C., Fusco, G., Licciardello, R. and Musso, A. (2017), "Rail freight network in Europe: Opportunities provided by re-launching the single wagonload system", *Transportation Research Procedia*, Vol. 25, pp. 5185–5204.

Guilbault, M. and Cruz, C. (2010), "Shippers mode choices and logistic constraints", *The 12th WCTR Proceedings, Lisbon, Portugal*.

Gunningham, N. and Sinclair, D. (1999), "Integrative regulation: a principle-based approach to environmental policy", *Law & Social Inquiry*, Vol. 24 No. 4, pp. 853–896.

Guo, W., van Blokland, W.B. and Lodewijks, G. (2017), "Survey on characteristics and challenges of synchromodal transportation in global cold chains", in Bektaş, T., Coniglio, S., Martinez-Sykora, A. and Voß, S. (Eds.), *Computational Logistics*, Springer International Publishing, Cham, pp. 420–434.

Hackbarth, A. and Madlener, R. (2013), "Consumer preferences for alternative fuel vehicles: A discrete choice analysis", *Transportation Research Part D: Transport and Environment*, Vol. 25, pp. 5–17.

Hardin, G. (1968), "The tragedy of the commons", *Science*, Vol. 162, pp. 1243–1248.

Hart, S.L. (1995), "A natural-resource-based view of the firm", *The Academy of Management Review*, Vol. 20 No. 4, p. 986.

Hart, S.L. and Dowell, G. (2011), "A natural-resource-based view of the firm: Fifteen years after", *Journal of Management*, Vol. 37 No. 5, pp. 1464–1479.

Hatch, M.J. (2018), *Organization theory: modern, symbolic, and postmodern perspectives*, Oxford University Press.

Hazen, B., Overstreet, R. and Wang, Y. (2015), "Predicting public bicycle adoption using the technology acceptance model", *Sustainability*, Vol. 7 No. 11, pp. 14558–14573.

Hernández, S., Peeta, S. and Kalafatas, G. (2011), "A less-than-truckload carrier collaboration planning problem under dynamic capacities", *Transportation Research Part E: Logistics and Transportation Review*, Vol. 47 No. 6, pp. 933–946.

Hofman, W., Punter, M., Bastiaansen, H., Cornelisse, E. and Dalmolen, S. (2016), "Semantic technology for enabling logistics innovations—towards intelligent cargo in the Physical Internet", *International Journal of Advanced Logistics*, Vol. 5 No. 2, pp. 58–69.

Holden, R.J. and Karsh, B.-T. (2010), "The Technology Acceptance Model: Its past and its future in health care", *Journal of Biomedical Informatics*, Vol. 43 No. 1, pp. 159–172.

Horbach, J., Rammer, C. and Rennings, K. (2012), "Determinants of eco-innovations by type of environmental impact—The role of regulatory push/pull, technology push and market pull", *Ecological Economics*, Vol. 78, pp. 112–122.

Howes, M., Wortley, L., Potts, R., Dedekorkut-Howes, A., Serrao-Neumann, S., Davidson, J., Smith, T. and Nunn, P. (2017), "Environmental Sustainability: A Case of Policy Implementation Failure?", *Sustainability*, Vol. 9 No. 2, p. 165.

Huang, G.Q. and Xu, S.X. (2013), "Truthful multi-unit transportation procurement auctions for logistics e-marketplaces", *Transportation Research Part B: Methodological*, Vol. 47, pp. 127–148.

Huijts, N., Molin, E. and van Wee, B. (2014), "Hydrogen fuel station acceptance. A structural equation model based on the technology acceptance framework", *Journal of Environmental Psychology*, Vol. 38, pp. 153–166.

Huizenga, C. and Leather, J. (2012), "Transport and climate policy in the developing world–the region that matters most", in Zachariadis, T. (Ed.), *Cars and carbon*, Springer, pp. 371–391.

Humphries, A.S. and Wilding, R.D. (2004), "Long term collaborative business relationships: The impact of trust and C 3 behaviour", *Journal of Marketing Management*, Vol. 20 No. 9–10, pp. 1107–1122.

Industry Commission (1998), *A Full Repairing Lease: Inquiry into Ecologically Sustainable Land Management. Report No 60*, Canberra.

International Transport Forum (2019), *ITF transport outlook 2019*, OECD Publishing, Paris.

Isaksson, K. and Huge-Brodin, M. (2013), "Understanding efficiencies behind logistics service providers' green offerings", *Management Research Review*, Vol. 36 No. 3, pp. 216–238.

Islam, D.M.Z., Ricci, S. and Nelldal, B.-L. (2016), "How to make modal shift from road to rail possible in the European transport market, as aspired to in the EU Transport White Paper 2011", *European Transport Research Review*, Vol. 8 No. 3, p. 18.

Jayaraman, Haron, H., Feng, C.K., Yusof, N. and Agbola, F. (2015), "Determinants of the intentionto use a natural gas vehicle (NGV) as an alternative to a petrol car. The case of Malaysia", *Journal of Sustainability, Science and Management*, Vol. 10 No. 1, pp. 36–49.

Jenkins, B. (2002), "Organisation for sustainability", *Australian Journal of Environmental Management*, Vol. 9 No. 4, pp. 243–251.

Ji, S., Peng, X. and Luo, R. (2019), "An integrated model for the production-inventory-distribution problem in the Physical Internet", *International Journal of Production Research*, Vol. 57 No. 4, pp. 1000–1017.

Kagermeier, A. (1998), "Nachhaltigkeitsdiskussion: Herausforderung für Verkehrsgeographie", *Geographische Rundschau*, Vol. 50, pp. 548–550.

Kang, M.J. and Park, H. (2011), "Impact of experience on government policy toward acceptance of hydrogen fuel cell vehicles in Korea", *Energy Policy*, Vol. 39 No. 6, pp. 3465–3475.

Karimi, B. and Bashiri, M. (2018), "Designing a multi-commodity multimodal splittable supply chain network by logistic hubs for intelligent manufacturing", *Procedia Manufacturing*, Vol. 17, pp. 1058–1064.

Kaye, S.-A., Lewis, I., Forward, S. and Delhomme, P. (2020), "A priori acceptance of highly automated cars in Australia, France, and Sweden: A theoretically-informed investigation guided by the TPB and UTAUT", *Accident Analysis & Prevention*, Vol. 137, pp. 1–11.

Kim, H.-C., Nicholson, A. and Kusumastuti, D. (2017), "Analysing freight shippers' mode choice preference heterogeneity using latent class modelling", *Transportation Research Procedia*, Vol. 25, pp. 1109–1125.

Kim, S.-T. and Lee, S.-Y. (2012), "Stakeholder pressure and the adoption of environmental logistics practices: is eco-oriented culture a missing link?", *The International Journal of Logistics Management*, Vol. 23 No. 2, pp. 238–258.

King, A. (2007), "Cooperation between corporations and environmental groups: A transaction cost perspective", *Academy of Management Review*, Vol. 32 No. 3, pp. 889–900.

Kluschke, P., Gnann, T., Plötz, P. and Wietschel, M. (2019), "Market diffusion of alternative fuels and powertrains in heavy-duty vehicles: A literature review", *Energy Reports*, Vol. 5, pp. 1010–1024.

Knol, A.J., Klievink, B. and Tan, Y.-H. (2014), "Data sharing issues and potential solutions for adoption of information infrastructures. Evidence from a data pipeline project in the global supply chain over sea", *Proceedings of the 27th Bled eConference*.

Kong, X.T., Chen, J., Luo, H. and Huang, G.Q. (2016), "Scheduling at an auction logistics centre with physical internet", *International Journal of Production Research*, Vol. 54 No. 9, pp. 2670–2690.

Kordnejad, B. (2014), "Intermodal transport cost model and intermodal distribution in urban freight", *Procedia—Social and Behavioral Sciences*, Vol. 125, pp. 358–372.

Kotzab, H., Darkow, I.-L., Bäumler, I., Georgi, C. and Luttermann, S. (2018), "Mapping Research on Logistics and Supply Chain Coordination, Cooperation and Collaboration", *Dynamics in Logistics*, pp. 10–20.

Kreutzberger, E. and Konings, R. (2016), "The challenge of appropriate hub terminal and hub-and-spoke network development for seaports and intermodal rail transport in Europe", *Research in Transportation Business & Management*, Vol. 19, pp. 83–96.

Krugman, P.R. and Wells, R. (2017), *Essentials of economics*, Fourth edition, Worth Publishers Macmillan Learning, New York.

Kumar, A. and Anbanandam, R. (2019), "Location selection of multimodal freight terminal under STEEP sustainability", *Research in Transportation Business & Management*, Vol. 33, p. 100434.

Kumar, A., Kwon, H.-T., Choi, K.-H., Lim, W., Cho, J.H., Tak, K. and Moon, I. (2011), "LNG: An eco-friendly cryogenic fuel for sustainable development", *Applied Energy*, Vol. 88 No. 12, pp. 4264–4273.

Kurapati, S., Kourounioti, I., Lukosch, H., Tavasszy, L. and Verbraeck, A. (2018), "Fostering sustainable transportation operations through corridor management. A simulation gaming approach", *Sustainability*, Vol. 10 No. 2, pp. 455–473.

Landschützer, C., Ehrentraut, F. and Jodin, D. (2015), "Containers for the Physical Internet. Requirements and engineering design related to FMCG logistics", *Logistics Research*, Vol. 8 No. 1, p. 8.

Landwehr, S. (2020), "Gas-LKW gefragter als gedacht", *Deutsche Verkehrs-Zeitung*, 5 May.

Langshaw, L., Ainalis, D., Acha, S., Shah, N. and Stettler, M.E.J. (2020), "Environmental and economic analysis of liquefied natural gas (LNG) for heavy goods vehicles in the UK: A Well-to-Wheel and total cost of ownership evaluation", *Energy Policy*, Vol. 137, p. 111161.

Layeb, S.B., Jaoua, A., Jbira, A. and Makhlouf, Y. (2018), "A simulation-optimization approach for scheduling in stochastic freight transportation", *Computers & Industrial Engineering*, Vol. 126, pp. 99–110.

Lazuras, L., Ketikidis, P. and Baresel-Bofinger, A. (2011), "Promoting green supply chain management: the role of the human factor", *15th Panhellenic Logistics Conference and 1st Southeast European Congress on Supply Chain Management, Thessaloniki, Greece*, pp. 1–13.

Le Li, Negenborn, R.R. and Schutter, B. de (2015), "Intermodal freight transport planning – a receding horizon control approach", *Transportation Research Part C: Emerging Technologies*, Vol. 60, pp. 77–95.

Ledyard, J.O. (2008), "Market failure", in Durlauf, S.N. and Blume, L.E. (Eds.), *The new Palgrave dictionary of economics*, Palgrave, McMillan, US.

Lee, Y., Kozar, K.A. and Larsen, K.R.T. (2003), "The technology acceptance model: Past, present, and future", *Communications of the Association for information systems*, Vol. 12 No. 1, p. 50.

Lemmens, N., Gijsbrechts, J. and Boute, R. (2019), "Synchromodality in the Physical Internet—dual sourcing and real-time switching between transport modes", *European Transport Research Review*, Vol. 11 No. 1, p. 19.

Li, J., Rong, G. and Feng, Y. (2015), "Request selection and exchange approach for carrier collaboration based on auction of a single request", *Transportation Research Part E: Logistics and Transportation Review*, Vol. 84, pp. 23–39.

Li, X. and Wang, W. (2018), "Study on the location of hub city based on container multimodal transport", in *CICTP 2017: Transportation Reform and Change—Equity, Inclusiveness, Sharing, and Innovation*, American Society of Civil Engineers Reston, VA, pp. 2866–2875.

Li, Y.Z. (2019), "Study of fire and explosion hazards of alternative fuel vehicles in tunnels", *Fire Safety Journal*, Vol. 110, p. 102871.

Lin, C.-Y. and Ho, Y.-H. (2011), "Determinants of green practice adoption for logistics companies in China", *Journal of Business Ethics*, Vol. 98 No. 1, pp. 67–83.

Lin, Y.-H., Meller, R.D., Ellis, K.P., Thomas, L.M. and Lombardi, B.J. (2014), "A decomposition-based approach for the selection of standardized modular containers", *International Journal of Production Research*, Vol. 52 No. 15, pp. 4660–4672.

Lindholm, M.E. and Blinge, M. (2014), "Assessing knowledge and awareness of the sustainable urban freight transport among Swedish local authority policy planners", *Transport Policy*, Vol. 32, pp. 124–131.

Liu, J., Feng, Y., Zhu, Q. and Sarkis, J. (2018), "Green supply chain management and the circular economy", *International Journal of Physical Distribution & Logistics Management*, Vol. 48 No. 8, pp. 794–817.

López-Navarro, M.Á., Ángel Moliner, M., María Rodríguez, R. and Sánchez, J. (2011), "Accompanied versus unaccompanied transport in short sea shipping between Spain and Italy: An Analysis from transport road firms perspective", *Transport Reviews*, Vol. 31 No. 4, pp. 425–444.

Lozano, R. (2008), "Envisioning sustainability three-dimensionally", *Journal of Cleaner Production*, Vol. 16 No. 17, pp. 1838–1846.

Lozano, R., Carpenter, A. and Huisingh, D. (2015), "A review of 'theories of the firm' and their contributions to Corporate Sustainability", *Journal of Cleaner Production*, Vol. 106, pp. 430–442.

Ma, L., Geng, J., Li, W., Liu, P. and Li, Z. (2013), "The development of natural gas as an automotive fuel in China", *Energy Policy*, Vol. 62, pp. 531–539.

Madden, T.J., Ellen, P.S. and Ajzen, I. (1992), "A comparison of the theory of planned behavior and the theory of reasoned action", *Personality and Social Psychology Bulletin*, Vol. 18 No. 1, pp. 3–9.

Márquez, L. and Cantillo, V. (2013), "Evaluating strategic freight transport corridors including external costs", *Transportation Planning and Technology*, Vol. 36 No. 6, pp. 529–546.

Martinsen, U. (2014), *Towards greener supply chains: inclusion of environmental activities in relationships between logistics service providers and shippers: Doctoral thesis*, Linköping University Electronic Press.

Mason, R., Lalwani, C. and Boughton, R. (2007), "Combining vertical and horizontal collaboration for transport optimisation", *Supply Chain Management: An International Journal*, Vol. 12 No. 3, pp. 187–199.

Matos, F.J. and Silva, F.J. (2011), "The rebound effect on road freight transport: Empirical evidence from Portugal", *Energy Policy*, Vol. 39 No. 5, pp. 2833–2841.

Mattauch, L., Ridgway, M. and Creutzig, F. (2016), "Happy or liberal? Making sense of behavior in transport policy design", *Transportation Research Part D: Transport and Environment*, Vol. 45 No. Supplement C, pp. 64–83.

Mauch, U., North, N. and Pulli, R. (2001), "Between efficiency and sufficiency. The optimal combination of policy instruments in the mobility sector towards sustainable development", in Kaufmann-Hayoz, R. and Gutscher, H. (Eds.), *Changing things—moving people: Strategies for promoting sustainable development at the local level*, Birkhäuser Basel, Basel, pp. 133–150.

McKinnon, A. (2018), *Decarbonizing logistics: Distributing goods in a low carbon world*, Kogan Page Publishers.

McKinnon, A., Browne, M., Whiteing, A. and Piecyk, M. (2015), *Green logistics: Improving the environmental sustainability of logistics*, Kogan Page Publishers.

Meinlschmidt, J., Schleper, M.C. and Foerstl, K. (2018), "Tackling the sustainability iceberg: a transaction cost economics approach to lower tier sustainability management", *International Journal of Operations & Production Management*, Vol. 38 No. 10, pp. 1888–1914.

Meixell, M.J. and Norbis, M. (2008), "A review of the transportation mode choice and carrier selection literature", *The International Journal of Logistics Management*, Vol. 19 No. 2, pp. 183–211.

Mickwitz, P. (2003), "A Framework for Evaluating Environmental Policy Instruments", *Evaluation*, Vol. 9 No. 4, pp. 415–436.

Monios, J. and Bergqvist, R. (2015), "Using a "virtual joint venture" to facilitate the adoption of intermodal transport", *Supply Chain Management: An International Journal*, Vol. 20 No. 5, pp. 534–548.

Montreuil, B. (2009), *Physical Internet manifesto: Globally transforming the way physical objects are handled, moved, stored, realized, supplied and used.*

Montreuil, B. (2011), "Toward a Physical Internet: meeting the global logistics sustainability grand challenge", *Logistics Research*, Vol. 3 No. 2–3, pp. 71–87.

Montreuil, B., Meller, R.D. and Ballot, E. (2013), "Physical Internet foundations", in Borangiu, T., Thomas, A. and Trentesaux, D. (Eds.), *Service orientation in holonic and multi agent manufacturing and robotics*, Springer Berlin Heidelberg, Berlin, Heidelberg, pp. 151–166.

Morales-Fusco, P., Grau, M. and Saurí, S. (2018), "Effects of RoPax shipping line strategies on freight price and transporter's choice. Policy implications for promoting MoS", *Transport Policy*, Vol. 67, pp. 67–76.

Morali, O. and Searcy, C. (2013), "A Review of Sustainable Supply Chain Management Practices in Canada", *Journal of Business Ethics*, Vol. 117 No. 3, pp. 635–658.

Morganti, E., Seidel, S., Blanquart, C., Dablanc, L. and Lenz, B. (2014), "The impact of e-commerce on final deliveries: alternative parcel delivery services in France and Germany", *Transportation Research Procedia*, Vol. 4, pp. 178–190.

Moriarty, P. and Honnery, D. (2019), "Prospects for hydrogen as a transport fuel", *International Journal of Hydrogen Energy*, Vol. 44 No. 31, pp. 16029–16037.

Mortimer, P. and Islam, D.M.Z. (2014), "A comparison of North American and European railway systems–a critique and riposte", *European Transport Research Review*, Vol. 6 No. 4, pp. 503–510.

Mostert, M. and Limbourg, S. (2016), "External costs as competitiveness factors for freight transport—a state of the art", *Transport Reviews*, Vol. 36 No. 6, pp. 692–712.

Muller, A. (2008), "Sufficiency–does energy consumption become a moral issue?", in Energy Science Center ETH Zürich (Ed.), *Smart energy strategies: Meeting the climate change challenge*, Wirtschaft, Energie, Umwelt, vdf Hochschulverlag, Zürich, pp. 86–88.

Nakamura, A.O., Tiessen, P. and Diewert, W.E. (2003), "Information failure as an alternative explanation of under investment in R&D", *Managerial and Decision Economics*, Vol. 24 No. 2/3, pp. 231–239.

Nielsen, J. (1993), *Usability engineering*, Morgan Kaufmann, Amsterdam.

O'Garra, T., Mourato, S. and Pearson, P. (2005), "Analysing awareness and acceptability of hydrogen vehicles. A London case study", *International Journal of Hydrogen Energy*, Vol. 30 No. 6, pp. 649–659.

Ogden, J., Jaffe, A.M., Scheitrum, D., McDonald, Z. and Miller, M. (2018), "Natural gas as a bridge to hydrogen transportation fuel: Insights from the literature", *Energy Policy*, Vol. 115, pp. 317–329.

Oliver, C. (1991), "Strategic responses to institutional processes", *Academy of Management Review*, Vol. 16 No. 1, pp. 145–179.

Opschoor, J.B. (1994), *Managing the environment: The role of economic instruments*, OECD, Paris.

Osorio-Mora, A., Núñez-Cerda, F., Gatica, G., Linfati, R. and Li, Z.-C. (2020), "Multimodal capacitated hub location problems with multi-commodities: an application in freight transport", *Journal of Advanced Transportation*, Vol. 2020, p. 2431763.

Osorio-Tejada, J.L., Llera, E. and Scarpellini, S. (2015), "LNG: an alternative fuel for road freight transport in Europe", *WIT Transactions on The Built Environment*, Vol. 168, pp. 235–246.

Osorio-Tejada, J.L., Llera-Sastresa, E. and Scarpellini, S. (2017), "Liquefied natural gas: Could it be a reliable option for road freight transport in the EU?", *Renewable and Sustainable Energy Reviews*, Vol. 71, pp. 785–795.

Pan, S., Nigrelli, M., Ballot, E., Sarraj, R. and Yang, Y. (2015), "Perspectives of inventory control models in the Physical Internet: A simulation study", *Computers & Industrial Engineering*, Vol. 84, pp. 122–132.

Pan, S., Trentesaux, D., Ballot, E. and Huang, G.Q. (2019), "Horizontal collaborative transport: survey of solutions and practical implementation issues", *International Journal of Production Research*, Vol. 57 No. 15–16, pp. 5340–5361.

(2016), "Paris Agreement", in *United Nations Treaty Collection*.

Payre, W., Cestac, J. and Delhomme, P. (2014), "Intention to use a fully automated car: Attitudes and a priori acceptability", *Transportation Research Part F: Traffic Psychology and Behaviour*, Vol. 27, pp. 252–263.

Perboli, G., Musso, S., Rosano, M., Tadei, R. and Godel, M. (2017), "Synchro-modality and slow steaming: New business perspectives in freight transportation", *Sustainability*, Vol. 9 No. 10, p. 1843.

Perman, R., Ma, Y., McGilvray, J. and Common, M. (2003), *Natural resource and environmental economics*, Pearson Education.

Peters-von Rosenstiel, D., Siegemund, S., Bünger, U., Schmidt, P., Weindorf, W., Wurster, R. and Zerhusen, J. (2015), *LNG in Germany: Liquefied natural gas and renewable methane in heavy-duty road transport*, Berlin.

Pfeffer, J. and Salancik, G.R. (1978), *The external control of organizations: A resource dependence perspective*, Harper & Row, New York.

Pfoser, S. (in press), "Developing user-centered measures to increase the share of multimodal freight transport", *Research in Transportation Business & Management*.

Pfoser, S., Aschauer, G., Simmer, L. and Schauer, O. (2016a), "Facilitating the implementation of LNG as an alternative fuel technology in landlocked Europe: A study from Austria", *Research in Transportation Business & Management*, Vol. 18, pp. 77–84.

Pfoser, S., Berger, T., Hauger, G., Berkowitsch, C., Schodl, R., Eitler, S., Markvica, K., Hu, B., Zajicek, J. and Prandtstetter, M. (2018a), "Integrating high-performance transport modes into synchromodal transport networks", in Freitag, M., Kotzab, H. and Pannek, J. (Eds.), *Dynamics in logistics: Proceedings of the 6th International Conference LDIC 2018, Bremen, Germany / Michael Freitag, Herbert Kotzab, Jurgen Pannek, editors, Lecture Notes in Logistics*, Vol. 16, Springer, Cham, Switzerland, pp. 109–115.

Pfoser, S., Jung, E. and Putz, L.-M. (2018b), "Same river same rules? Administrative barriers in the Danube countries", *Journal of Sustainable Development of Transport and Logistics*, Vol. 3 No. 6.

Pfoser, S., Kotzab, H. and Bäumler, I. (in press), "Antecedents, mechanisms and effects of synchromodal freight transport: a conceptual framework from a systematic literature review", *The International Journal of Logistics Management*.

Pfoser, S., Putz, L.-M. and Jung, E. (2020), "Recommendations for human resources development in Danube inland ports", in Freitag, M., Haasis, H.-D., Kotzab, H. and Pannek, J. (Eds.), *Dynamics in Logistics, 2020, Cham*, Springer International Publishing, Cham, pp. 3–20.

Pfoser, S., Putz, L.-M., Schauer, O. and Kotzab, H. (2018c), "Exploring logistics managers' preferences for sustainable freight transport: a literature review on choice experiments", *Proceedings of the 7th Transport Research Arena*, pp. 1–8.

Pfoser, S., Schauer, O. and Costa, Y. (2018d), "Acceptance of LNG as an alternative fuel: Determinants and policy implications", *Energy Policy*, Vol. 120, pp. 259–267.

Pfoser, S., Treiblmaier, H. and Schauer, O. (2016b), "Critical success factors of synchromodality: Results from a case study and literature review", *Transportation Research Procedia*, Vol. 14, pp. 1463–1471.

Pindyck, R.S. and Rubinfeld, D.L. (2013), *Microeconomics, The Pearson series in economics*, Eighth edition, Pearson Education, Inc, Boston.

Plasch, M., Pfoser, S., Gerschberger, M., Schauer, O. and Gattringer, R. (2021), "Why collaborate in a Physical Internet network?—Motives and success factors", *Journal of Business Logistics*, Vol. 42 No. 1, pp. 120–143.

Pomponi, F., Fratocchi, L. and Rossi Tafuri, S. (2015), "Trust development and horizontal collaboration in logistics: a theory based evolutionary framework", *Supply Chain Management: An International Journal*, Vol. 20 No. 1, pp. 83–97.

Posset, M., Gierlinger, D., Gronalt, M., Peherstorfer, H., Pripfl, H. and Starkl, F. (2014), *Handbuch Intermodaler Verkehr Europa*, Steyr.

Pratt, R.M. and Phillips, P.S. (2000), "The role and success of UK waste minimisation clubs in the correction of market and information failures", *Resources, Conservation and Recycling*, Vol. 30 No. 3, pp. 201–219.

Puettmann, C. and Stadtler, H. (2010), "A collaborative planning approach for intermodal freight transportation", *OR Spectrum*, Vol. 32 No. 3, pp. 809–830.

Punte, S., Tavasszy, L., Baeyens, A. and Liesa, F. (2019), *A framework and process for the development of a roadmap towards zero emissions logistics 2050*.

Putz, L.-M., Treiblmaier, H. and Pfoser, S. (2018), "Field trips for sustainable transport education", *The International Journal of Logistics Management*.

Qiao, B., Pan, S. and Ballot, E. (2018), "Revenue optimization for less-than-truckload carriers in the Physical Internet: dynamic pricing and request selection", *Computers & Industrial Engineering*.

Qiao, B., Pan, S. and Ballot, E. (2019), "Dynamic pricing model for less-than-truckload carriers in the Physical Internet", *Journal of Intelligent Manufacturing*, Vol. 30 No. 7, pp. 2631–2643.

Ramachandran, S. and Stimming, U. (2015), "Well to wheel analysis of low carbon alternatives for road traffic", *Energy & Environmental Science*, Vol. 8 No. 11, pp. 3313–3324.

Reichel, J. (2020), "Shell: Anlage für Bio-LNG soll CO2-freien Transport ermöglichen", *Logistra*, 12 May.

Reis, V. (2015), "Should we keep on renaming a +35-year-old baby?", *Journal of Transport Geography*, Vol. 46, pp. 173–179.

Reis, V., Meier, F.J., Pace, G. and Palacin, R. (2013), "Rail and multi-modal transport", *Research in Transportation Economics*, Vol. 41 No. 1, pp. 17–30.

Reusswig, F., Gerlinger, K. and Edenhofer, O. (2004), *Lebensstile und globaler Energieverbrauch: Analyse und Strategieansätze zu einer nachhaltigen Energiestruktur, PIK Report Nr. 90*, Potsdam Institut für Klimafolgenforschung, Potsdam.

Richardson, B.C. (2005), "Sustainable transport: analysis frameworks", *Journal of Transport Geography*, Vol. 13 No. 1, pp. 29–39.

Risser, R. and Lehner, U. (1998), "Acceptability of speeds and speed limits to drivers and pedestrians/cyclists", *Master Deliverable*, Vol. 6.

Rivera, J. (2004), "Institutional pressures and voluntary environmental behavior in developing countries: Evidence from the Costa Rican hotel industry", *Society and Natural Resources*, Vol. 17 No. 9, pp. 779–797.

Rodrigue, J.-P. and Notteboom, T. (2010), "Comparative North American and European gateway logistics: the regionalism of freight distribution", *Journal of Transport Geography*, Vol. 18 No. 4, pp. 497–507.

Rodrigues, V.S., Harris, I. and Mason, R. (2015), "Horizontal logistics collaboration for enhanced supply chain performance: An international retail perspective", *Supply Chain Management: An International Journal*, Vol. 20, pp. 631–647.

Ronteltap, A., van Trijp, J.C. and Renes, R.J. (2008), "Consumer acceptance of nutrigenomics-based personalised nutrition", *British Journal of Nutrition*, Vol. 101 No. 1, pp. 132–144.

Rosen, C.M., Beckman, S.L. and Bercovitz, J. (2002), "The role of voluntary industry standards in environmental supply-chain management: an institutional economics perspective", *Journal of Industrial Ecology*, Vol. 6 No. 3-4, pp. 103–123.

Saad, F. (2004), "Behavioural adaptations to new support systems—some critical issues", *Proceedings of the IEEE International Conference on Systems, Man, and Cybernetics*, pp. 288–293.

Sadvandi, S. and Halkias, D. (2019), "Challenges of human factors engineering in the coming transition to autonomous vehicle technologies: A multiple case study", *The ISM Journal of International Business*, Vol. 3 No. 1, pp. 3–8.

Sáenz, M. (2016), *The Physical Internet: Logistics reimagined?*

Šakalys, R. and Batarlienė, N. (2017), "Research on intermodal terminal interaction in international transport corridors", *Procedia Engineering*, Vol. 187, pp. 281–288.

Sallez, Y., Montreuil, B. and Ballot, E. (2015), "On the activeness of Physical Internet containers", in Borangiu, T., Thomas, A. and Trentesaux, D. (Eds.), *Service Orientation in Holonic and Multi-agent Manufacturing*, Springer International Publishing, Cham, pp. 259–269.

Samadi, S., Gröne, M.-C., Schneidewind, U., Luhmann, H.-J., Venjakob, J. and Best, B. (2017), "Sufficiency in energy scenario studies: Taking the potential benefits of lifestyle changes into account", *Technological Forecasting and Social Change*, Vol. 124, pp. 126–134.

Sancha, C., Longoni, A. and Giménez, C. (2015), "Sustainable supplier development practices: Drivers and enablers in a global context", *Journal of Purchasing and Supply Management*, Vol. 21 No. 2, pp. 95–102.

Sanchez Rodrigues, V., Harris, I. and Mason, R. (2015), "Horizontal logistics collaboration for enhanced supply chain performance: an international retail perspective", *Supply Chain Management: An International Journal*, Vol. 20 No. 6, pp. 631–647.

Sang, Y.-N. and Bekhet, H.A. (2015), "Modelling electric vehicle usage intentions: an empirical study in Malaysia", *Journal of Cleaner Production*, Vol. 92, pp. 75–83.

Sarkis, J., Zhu, Q. and Lai, K. (2011), "An organizational theoretic review of green supply chain management literature", *International Journal of Production Economics*, Vol. 130 No. 1, pp. 1–15.

Sarraj, R., Ballot, E., Pan, S. and Montreuil, B. (2014), "Analogies between Internet network and logistics service networks: challenges involved in the interconnection", *Journal of Intelligent Manufacturing*, Vol. 25 No. 6, pp. 1207–1219.

Scania (2020), "Gas geben und richtig sparen", available at: https://www.scania.com/de/de/
home/experience-scania/Zufriedene-Kunden/westfalen-lippe-spedition-begeistert-von-
Ing-lkw-von-scania-.html.

Schade, J. and Baum, M. (2007), "Reactance or acceptance? Reactions towards the introduction of road pricing", *Transportation Research Part A: Policy and Practice*, Vol. 41 No. 1,
pp. 41–48.

Scheitrum, D., Myers Jaffe, A., Dominguez-Faus, R. and Parker, N. (2017), "California low
carbon fuel policies and natural gas fueling infrastructure: Synergies and challenges to
expanding the use of RNG in transportation", *Energy Policy*, Vol. 110, pp. 355–364.

Schepers, J. and Wetzels, M. (2007), "A meta-analysis of the technology acceptance model:
Investigating subjective norm and moderation effects", *Information & management*,
Vol. 44 No. 1, pp. 90–103.

Schmalfuß, F., Mühl, K. and Krems, J.F. (2017), "Direct experience with battery electric
vehicles (BEVs) matters when evaluating vehicle attributes, attitude and purchase intention", *Transportation Research Part F: Traffic Psychology and Behaviour*, Vol. 46,
pp. 47–69.

Schmid, D. and Graf, R. (2016), "The acceptance of different perspectives in a synthetic
vision navigation display", *Proceedings of the International Conference on Human-
Computer Interaction in Aerospace*, pp. 1–8.

Schrettle, S., Hinz, A., Scherrer-Rathje, M. and Friedli, T. (2014), "Turning sustainability into action: Explaining firms' sustainability efforts and their impact on firm performance", *International Journal of Production Economics*, Vol. 147, pp. 73–84.

Schulte, I., Hart, D. and van der Vorst, R. (2004), "Issues affecting the acceptance of hydrogen fuel", *International Journal of Hydrogen Energy*, Vol. 29 No. 7, pp. 677–685.

Scott, W.R. (1987), "The adolescence of institutional theory", *Administrative Science Quarterly*, Vol. 32 No. 4, pp. 493–511.

Sen, S. and Cowley, J. (2013), "The relevance of stakeholder theory and social capital theory
in the context of CSR in SMEs: An Australian perspective", *Journal of Business Ethics*,
Vol. 118 No. 2, pp. 413–427.

Shang, K.-C., Lu, C.-S. and Li, S. (2010), "A taxonomy of green supply chain management capability among electronics-related manufacturing firms in Taiwan", *Journal of
Environmental Management*, Vol. 91 No. 5, pp. 1218–1226.

Shangbing, Y. (2009), "Technology and system maintenance of liquefied natural gas vehicle", *Chemical Engineering of Oil & Gas*, Vol. 5.

Sheu, J.-B. and Chen, Y.J. (2012), "Impact of government financial intervention on competition among green supply chains", *International Journal of Production Economics*,
Vol. 138 No. 1, pp. 201–213.

Shi, R. and Li, Z. (2010), "Pricing of multimodal transportation networks under different market regimes", *Journal of Transportation Systems Engineering and Information
Technology*, Vol. 10 No. 5, pp. 91–97.

Simeonova, K. and Diaz-Bone, H. (2005), "Integrated climate-change strategies of industrialized countries", *Energy*, Vol. 30 No. 14, pp. 2537–2557.

Simio, L. de, Gambino, M. and Iannaccone, S. (2013), "Possible transport energy sources for
the future", *Transport Policy*, Vol. 27, pp. 1–10.

Singh, P.M. and van Sinderen, M. (2015), "Interoperability challenges for context aware logistics services-the case of synchromodal logistics", *Proceedings of the Workshops of the 6th International IFIP Working Conference on Enterprise Interoperability*, Vol. 1414, pp. 1–9.

Sinnandavar, C.M., Wong, W.-P. and Soh, K.-L. (2018), "Dynamics of supply environment and information system: Integration, green economy and performance", *Special Issue on Climate Change and Transport*, Vol. 62, pp. 536–550.

Smith, A.S.J., Benedetto, V. and Nash, C. (2018), "The impact of economic regulation on the efficiency of European railway systems", *Journal of Transport Economics and Policy*, Vol. 52 No. 2, pp. 113–136.

Song, H., Ou, X., Yuan, J., Yu, M. and Wang, C. (2017), "Energy consumption and greenhouse gas emissions of diesel/LNG heavy-duty vehicle fleets in China based on a bottom-up model analysis", *Energy*, Vol. 140, pp. 966–978.

Staats, H. (2004), "Pro-environmental attitudes and behavioral change", in Spielberger, C.D. (Ed.), *Encyclopedia of Applied Psychology*, Elsevier, New York, pp. 127–135.

Stank, T., Autry, C., Daugherty, P. and Closs, D. (2015), "Reimagining the 10 megatrends that will revolutionize supply chain logistics", *Transportation Journal*, Vol. 54 No. 1, pp. 7–32.

SteadieSeifi, M., Dellaert, N.P., Nuijten, W., van Woensel, T. and Raoufi, R. (2014), "Multimodal freight transportation planning. A literature review", *European Journal of Operational Research*, Vol. 233 No. 1, pp. 1–15.

Sternberg, H. and Norrman, A. (2017), "The Physical Internet–review, analysis and future research agenda", *International Journal of Physical Distribution & Logistics Management*, Vol. 47 No. 8, pp. 736–762.

Szyliowicz, J.S. (2003), "Decision-making, intermodal transportation, and sustainable mobility: towards a new paradigm", *International Social Science Journal*, Vol. 55 No. 176, pp. 185–197.

Tarigan, A.K., Bayer, S.B., Langhelle, O. and Thesen, G. (2012), "Estimating determinants of public acceptance of hydrogen vehicles and refuelling stations in greater Stavanger", *International Journal of Hydrogen Energy*, Vol. 37 No. 7, pp. 6063–6073.

Taylor, C., Pollard, S., Rocks, S. and Angus, A. (2012), "Selecting policy instruments for better environmental regulation: a critique and future research agenda", *Environmental Policy and Governance*, Vol. 22 No. 4, pp. 268–292.

Taylor, M. (2008), "Beyond technology-push and demand-pull: Lessons from California's solar policy", *Energy Economics*, Vol. 30 No. 6, pp. 2829–2854.

Thesen, G. and Langhelle, O. (2008), "Awareness, acceptability and attitudes towards hydrogen vehicles and filling stations. A Greater Stavanger case study and comparisons with London", *International Journal of Hydrogen Energy*, Vol. 33 No. 21, pp. 5859–5867.

Thrän, D., Billig, E., Persson, T., Svensson, M., Daniel-Gromke, J., Ponitka, J. and Seiffert, M. (2014), *Biomethane: Status and factors affecting market development and trade.*

Touboulic, A. and Walker, H. (2015), "Theories in sustainable supply chain management: a structured literature review", *International Journal of Physical Distribution & Logistics Management*, Vol. 45 No. 1, pp. 16–42.

Tran-Dang, H., Krommenacker, N. and Charpentier, P. (2017), "Containers monitoring through the Physical Internet: a spatial 3D model based on wireless sensor networks", *International Journal of Production Research*, Vol. 55 No. 9, pp. 2650–2663.

Ulrich, D. and Barney, J.B. (1984), "Perspectives in organizations: resource dependence, efficiency, and population", *Academy of Management Review*, Vol. 9 No. 3, pp. 471–481.

UN/ECE, ECMT, EC, United Nations (2001), *Terminology of combined transport*, New York, Geneva.

UNCTAD (1980), *Final act and convention on international multimodal transport of goods*, New York, Geneva.

van der Horst, M.R. and Langen, P.W. de (2008), "Coordination in hinterland transport chains. A major challenge for the seaport community", *Maritime Economics & Logistics*, Vol. 10 No. 1, pp. 108–129.

van der Vorst, J., Ossevoort, R., Keizer, M. de, van Woensel, T., Verdouw, C.N., Wenink, E., Koppes, R. and van Willegen, R. (2016), "DAVINC3I: Towards collaborative responsive logistics networks in floriculture", in Zijm, H., Klumpp, M., Clausen, U. and Hompel, M.t. (Eds.), *Logistics and Supply Chain innovation: Bridging the Gap between Theory and Practice*, Springer International Publishing, Cham, pp. 37–53.

van Essen, H., van Wijngaarden, L., Schroten, A., Sutter, D., Bieler, C., Maffii, S., Brambilla, M., Fiorello, D., Fermi, F., Parolin, R. and El Beyrouty, K. (2019), *Handbook on the external costs of transport*, Luxembourg.

van Hoof, B. and Lyon, T.P. (2013), "Cleaner production in small firms taking part in Mexico's Sustainable Supplier Program", *Journal of Cleaner Production*, Vol. 41, pp. 270–282.

van Leijen, M. (2018), "2018: the year of multimodality, masterplans and strikes", *Railfreight.com*, 31 December.

van Riessen, B., Negenborn, R.R. and Dekker, R. (2015), "Synchromodal container transportation: an overview of current topics and research opportunities", in Corman, F., Voß, S. and Negenborn, R.R. (Eds.), *Computational Logistics: 6th International Conference, ICCL 2015, Delft, The Netherlands, September 23–25, 2015, Proceedings*, Springer International Publishing, Cham, pp. 386–397.

van Riessen, B., Negenborn, R.R. and Dekker, R. (2017), "The Cargo Fare Class Mix problem for an intermodal corridor. Revenue management in synchromodal container transportation", *Flexible Services and Manufacturing Journal*, Vol. 29 No. 3-4, pp. 634–658.

van Rijnsoever, F.J., Hagen, P. and Willems, M. (2013), "Preferences for alternative fuel vehicles by Dutch local governments", *Transportation Research Part D: Transport and Environment*, Vol. 20, pp. 15–20.

Vanem, E., Antao, P., Ostvik, I. and Del Castillo de Comas, Francisco (2008), "Analysing the risk of LNG carrier operations", *Reliability Engineering & System Safety*, Vol. 93 No. 9, pp. 1328–1344.

Vanovermeire, C., Sörensen, K., van Breedam, A., Vannieuwenhuyse, B. and Verstrepen, S. (2014), "Horizontal logistics collaboration: decreasing costs through flexibility and an adequate cost allocation strategy", *International Journal of Logistics Research and Applications*, Vol. 17 No. 4, pp. 339–355.

Vedung, E. (2010), "Policy instruments: typologies and theories", in Vedung, E. (Ed.), *Carrots, sticks & sermons: Policy instruments and their evaluation*, 5th ed., Routledge, New York, pp. 21–58.

Venkatadri, U., Krishna, K.S. and Ülkü, M.A. (2016), "On Physical Internet logistics: modeling the impact of consolidation on transportation and inventory costs", *IEEE Transactions on Automation Science and Engineering*, Vol. 13 No. 4, pp. 1517–1527.

via donau (2019), *Manual on Danube navigation*, 4th ed., Viadonau–Österreichische Wasserstraßen Ges. mbH., Vienna.

Völklein, M. (2019), "Auch mit Gas-Antrieb sind Lkws nicht wirklich sauber", *Süddeutsche Zeitung*, 11 October.

Vollenbroek, F.A. (2002), "Sustainable development and the challenge of innovation", *Journal of Cleaner Production*, Vol. 10 No. 3, pp. 215–223.

Walha, F., Bekrar, A., Chaabane, S. and Loukil, T.M. (2016), "A rail-road PI-hub allocation problem: Active and reactive approaches", *Computers in Industry*, Vol. 81, pp. 138–151.

Wang, H., Fang, H., Yu, X. and Wang, K. (2015), "Development of natural gas vehicles in China. An assessment of enabling factors and barriers", *Energy Policy*, Vol. 85 No. Supplement C, pp. 80–93.

Wang, S., Fan, J., Zhao, D., Yang, S. and Fu, Y. (2016), "Predicting consumers' intention to adopt hybrid electric vehicles: using an extended version of the theory of planned behavior model", *Transportation*, Vol. 43 No. 1, pp. 123–143.

Wang, Y., Wang, S., Wang, J., Wei, J. and Wang, C. (2018), "An empirical study of consumers' intention to use ride-sharing services: using an extended technology acceptance model", *Transportation*, pp. 1–19.

Wang, Z. and Lu, M. (2014), "An empirical study of direct rebound effect for road freight transport in China", *Applied Energy*, Vol. 133, pp. 274–281.

Weber, M., Driessen, P.P. and Runhaar, H.A. (2014), "Evaluating environmental policy instruments mixes. A methodology illustrated by noise policy in the Netherlands", *Journal of Environmental Planning and Management*, Vol. 57 No. 9, pp. 1381–1397.

Wernerfelt, B. (1984), "A resource-based view of the firm", *Strategic Management Journal*, Vol. 5 No. 2, pp. 171–180.

Wiens, J., Powars, C. and Pope, G. (2001), "LNG vehicle fuel pressure strategy alternatives", *SAE Transactions*, pp. 1098–1112.

Williamson, O.E. (1981), "The economics of organization: The transaction cost approach", *American Journal of Sociology*, Vol. 87 No. 3, pp. 548–577.

Wittenbrink, P. (2015), Green Logistics: Konzept, aktuelle Entwicklungen und Handlungsfelder zur Emissionsreduktion im Transportbereich, Springer-Verlag.

Wolfinger, D., Tricoire, F. and Doerner, K.F. (2019), "A matheuristic for a multimodal long haul routing problem", *EURO Journal on Transportation and Logistics*, Vol. 8 No. 4, pp. 397–433.

World Commission on Environment and Development (1987), *Our common future*, Oxford University Press, Oxford.

Wu, L.-Y. (2010), "Applicability of the resource-based and dynamic-capability views under environmental volatility", *Journal of Business Research*, Vol. 63 No. 1, pp. 27–31.

Xiaodong, Y.Y. and Wang Shunhua, Y. (2009), "Self-pressurization and gas supplying properties of storage system for LNG vehicle", *Cryogenics*, Vol. 4.

Xie, C.S., Li, G. and Chang, Q. (2007), "Comparison among LNG, CNG and l-CNG filling stations", *Gas & Heat*, Vol. 7, pp. 6–12.

Xu, Z., Zhang, K., Min, H., Wang, Z., Zhao, X. and Liu, P. (2018), "What drives people to accept automated vehicles? Findings from a field experiment", *Transportation Research Part C: Emerging Technologies*, Vol. 95, pp. 320–334.

Xunmin, O. (2019), "Life Cycle Analysis on Liquefied Natural Gas and Compressed Natural Gas in Heavy-duty Trucks with Methane Leakage Emphasized", *Energy Procedia*, Vol. 158, pp. 3652–3657.

Yang, C.-S. (2018), "An analysis of institutional pressures, green supply chain management, and green performance in the container shipping context", *Transportation Research Part D: Transport and Environment*, Vol. 61, pp. 246–260.

Yang, Y., Pan, S. and Ballot, E. (2017), "Innovative vendor-managed inventory strategy exploiting interconnected logistics services in the Physical Internet", *International Journal of Production Research*, Vol. 55 No. 9, pp. 2685–2702.

Yeh, S. (2007), "An empirical analysis on the adoption of alternative fuel vehicles: The case of natural gas vehicles", *Energy Policy*, Vol. 35 No. 11, pp. 5865–5875.

Yonggang, W., Yunwen, C., Shuanshi, F., Chengming, A. and Wendong, X. (2013), "Development of LNG vehicles technology and its prospect of popularization and application", *Chemical Engineering of Oil & Gas*, Vol. 42 No. 3.

Yuen, K.F., Wang, X., Wong, Y.D. and Zhou, Q. (2017), "Antecedents and outcomes of sustainable shipping practices: The integration of stakeholder and behavioural theories", *Transportation Research Part E: Logistics and Transportation Review*, Vol. 108, pp. 18–35.

Zachariah-Wolff, J.L. and Hemmes, K. (2006), "Public Acceptance of Hydrogen in the Netherlands. Two Surveys That Demystify Public Views on a Hydrogen Economy", *Bulletin of Science, Technology & Society*, Vol. 26 No. 4, pp. 339–345.

Zhang, X., Myhrvold, N.P., Hausfather, Z. and Caldeira, K. (2016), "Climate benefits of natural gas as a bridge fuel and potential delay of near-zero energy systems", *Applied Energy*, Vol. 167, pp. 317–322.

Zhang, Y., Yu, Y. and Zou, B. (2011), "Analyzing public awareness and acceptance of alternative fuel vehicles in China. The case of EV", *Energy Policy*, Vol. 39 No. 11, pp. 7015–7024.

Zheng, N., Rérat, G. and Geroliminis, N. (2016), "Time-dependent area-based pricing for multimodal systems with heterogeneous users in an agent-based environment", *Transportation Research Part C: Emerging Technologies*, Vol. 62, pp. 133–148.

Zhou, C. (2011), "Code Selection and Design of LNG Filling Station", *Gas & Heat*, Vol. 5.

Zhu, Q., Sarkis, J. and Lai, K. (2013), "Institutional-based antecedents and performance outcomes of internal and external green supply chain management practices", *Journal of Purchasing and Supply Management*, Vol. 19 No. 2, pp. 106–117.

Zhu, S. (2011), "Fire protection design of LNG vehicle refueling station", *Fire Science and Technology*, Vol. 6.

Ziefle, M., Beul-Leusmann, S., Zaunbrecher, B.S. and Kasugai, K. (2015), "Integrating the "E" in Public Transport", in Giaffreda, R. (Ed.), *Internet of things: IoT infrastructures First International Summit, IoT360 2014, Rome, Italy, October 27–28, 2014, Revised Selected Papers, Lecture Notes of the Institute for Computer Sciences, Social Informatics and Telecommunications Engineering*, Vol. 151, Springer, Cham, New York, pp. 150–156.

Zijm, H. and Klumpp, M. (2016), "Logistics and supply chain management: developments and trends", in Zijm, H., Klumpp, M., Clausen, U. and Hompel, M.t. (Eds.), *Logistics and Supply Chain innovation: Bridging the Gap between Theory and Practice*, Springer International Publishing, Cham, pp. 1–20.

The manufacturer's authorised representative in the EU is Springer
Nature Customer Service Centre GmbH, Europaplatz 3, 69115 Heidelberg,
Germany. If you have any concerns regarding our products, please
contact ProductSafety@springernature.com

Printed and bound by CPI Group (UK) Ltd, Croydon, CR0 4YY
28/04/2026
02098535-0002